*Before **Heaven**: Hints Tips Stories*
Bryan Foster

*Before **Heaven**: Hints Tips Stories*
Bryan Foster

Before **Heaven**: *Hints Tips Stories*
Bryan Foster

Before

Heaven

Before **Heaven**: *Hints Tips Stories*
Bryan Foster

Before Heaven

Hints Tips Stories

Bryan Foster

Book 9 of the 10 Book

'GOD Today' Series

*Before **Heaven**: Hints Tips Stories*
Bryan Foster

Published in 2023

'God Today' Series. 10 Book Series. (2016-2023)

Great Developments Publishers
(Bryan Foster and Karen Foster, Directors)
Gold Coast, Queensland, Australia 4217
ACN: 33435168 ABN: 13133435168 USA-EIN: 98-0689457

All rights reserved. No part of this publication may be reproduced, stored in a retrieval system, transmitted in any form or by any means, electronic, mechanical, photocopying, recording, or otherwise, without the prior permission of the publisher and copyright holders. The author and publisher disclaim liability for any use, misuse, or misunderstanding of any information contained herein or for any loss, damage, or injury (be it health, financial, or otherwise) for any individual or group acting upon or relying on information contained or inferred from this work.

The moral rights of the author have been asserted.

Copyright © Great Developments Publishers, Bryan W. Foster and Karen M. Foster, Directors, 2023.

Creator: Foster, Bryan – author, editor, publishing director

Artwork – Bryan Foster and Bookpod

Title: *Before Heaven*

ISBN:978-0-6452220-2-9	(hardback)
ISBN:978-0-6452220-3-6	(paperback)
ISBN:978-0-6452220-4-3	(eBook)
ISBN:978-0-6452220-5-0	(large print paperback)

*Before **Heaven**: Hints Tips Stories*
Bryan Foster

NOT AI-ASSISTED. Publishers and Author Overseen

Notes: Includes Bibliographical References + Content Topics + Content Details + Overviews

'GOD Today' Series x10 Books
Author: Bryan Foster
Series Compiled: 2016-2023

info@bryanfosterauthor.com

1. *1God.world: One God for All* (2016)

2. *Mt Warning God's Revelations: Photobook Companion to '1God.world'* (2017)

3. *Where's God? Revelations Today* (2018)

4. *Where's God? Revelations Today Photobook Companion: GOD Signs (2nd ed)* (2018)

5. *Jesus and *Mahomad are God* (2020)

6. *Love is the Meaning of Life: GOD'S Love* (2021)

7. *Wisdom: God's Hints and Tips* (2021)

8. *Love is the Meaning of Life* (2022) (An introduction for secular people)

9. *Before Heaven: Hints Tips Stories* (2023)

10. *Before Heaven: Hints Tips Stories* (2nd ed) (2023)

*Before **Heaven**: Hints Tips Stories*
Bryan Foster

V. *GOD Today Video Series* (2018) (30+ free videos at this stage.) (Plus 750+ for all other series and topics; @ CaravanAus and efozz1 on YouTube)

(* N.B. This spelling of *Mahomad throughout the *Series* is deliberate. It is how God spelled it, except once, in the Revelations to the author in 2016.)

Author's Key Websites for this Series

https://www.godtodayseries.com/

https://www.bryanfosterauthor.com/

https://www.facebook.com/groups/389602698051426/

https://www.jesusandmahomadaregod.com/ (Developing)

'GOD Today' Series
2016-2023
Cover Images and Photobooks

Bryan W. Foster and Karen M. Foster (GDP)

Andrew Foster (Austographer.com/Photographic Consultant)

*Before **Heaven**: Hints Tips Stories*
Bryan Foster

Great Developments Publishers (GDP)

info@bryanfosterauthor.com

info@godtodayseries.com

Graphics and artwork: Bryan Foster and Bookpod

Before **Heaven**: *Hints Tips Stories*
Bryan Foster

Dedication

I dedicate this Book 9 *Before Heaven: Challenges from God* in the *'God Today' Series* to my deceased father, mother, and family. Karen, the Love of my life, and my wife of 45 years. My angel, my rock, my Uluru, my heart of Australia.

To my loving children Leigh-Maree, Andrew, Jacqueline, and daughter-in-law Shannon, Grandchildren Kyan, Cruze, Felicity, and Isabella.

And to my siblings John, Sooz, and Clare, and all my extended family.

Thank you for all your Love, support, and encouragement over these many years.

Along with my dear friends and former colleagues, thank you for your highly valued and generous support and encouragement for decades.

*Before **Heaven**: Hints Tips Stories*
Bryan Foster

Contents

Unique Images from God, Foreword, Preface	12
Introduction	21
Highlighted Book 9 Themes Introduced	31
Only One God + One Religion forever. In the transition era	36
God Asked Author to be His Prophet	45
Physical Evidence of God	50
Other Unique Photographic Images from God	64
Challenges At and After Death	77
Humans, Plants, Animals + maybe inert creations - Go to Heaven	82
Medical Issues + Disclaimer	86
God - Primary Bibliographical Source for Series	97
Jesus and Mahomad – Are Both God Incarnate	101
Hell = Absolute Evil and Total Isolation Forever! Who Goes There?	117
SO MASSIVE. SO CHALLENGING. SO GOD. This Is It!?	142
'God Today' Series 10 Books' Overviews	163
Conclusion	172
Bibliography	180

Before **Heaven**: *Hints Tips Stories*
Bryan Foster

Contents - Detailed	185
Author's Top 22 Revelations and Inspired Messages for Today	– 193
Beauty, God and Us	201
God. Angels. Feathers - An Overview.	210
Author's Publications 2007-2023	212
Author's Websites (Live plus Drafts) + Overview of Author	216
Publisher	218

Unique Images from God

p.63 Bryan at Rainforest Park Mt Warning camping ground in 2018. A sun arrow is seen across the chest, coming from a faint sun flare.

p.65 Bryan near the walkers' car park at the foot of the Mt Warning/Wollumbin hike in 2018. Two sun arrow images coming from a sun flare and then going across my neck and chest.

p.67 Giant Easter Sun Cross formed over a series of 6 photos at Texas on the Qld/NSW border in far north NSW in 2018

Image of the original Revelation #15 written down by the author as directed by God in 2016, while camping in the Murwillumbah Show Grounds.

(See Book 4 in this Series for many other Unique and/or spectacular images, some in photographic series. *Where's God? Revelations Today Photobook Companion: GOD Signs (2nd ed)*, 2018 by Bryan Foster)

*Before **Heaven**: Hints Tips Stories*
Bryan Foster

Background Information on these Images.

Most images in this Book 9 and Book 4 were taken in 2018 on my mobile cell phone. Not using cameras with shutters, etc.

There are a considerable number of other images from different venues within my geographical region, mostly on or about the volcanic rim of Mt Warning/Wollumbin. These were mostly taken that same year.

No photographer has yet offered a reasonable description of how these images were formed from a physical, photographic angle. Mobile phones have their own unique process of taking images.

Book 4 is a photobook concentrating on mostly Unique sun arrow images coming from a sun flare mostly shining through a rainforest canopy. All were taken by Bryan.

He strongly believes in the authenticity of each image. No outside software of any description was used e.g. No Photoshopping; just untouched phone images. I believe God is using these images and others to encourage the author (and probably others worldwide) to continue writing this Series and sharing the images worldwide, across all religions and cultures.

*Before **Heaven**: Hints Tips Stories*
Bryan Foster

Foreword by Karen Foster

Bryan has been challenged to explore and find the real, One and Only God for many years. I have witnessed this first-hand as he helps others, including myself, to see God personally in our lives. You are invited to explore these affirming messages from God for today's world. This is so special for everyone worldwide.

There seem to be three major camps of humanity when it comes to God these days in today's world. The first group is the believers in God. God's Absolute Love is for all people equally. Those unsure about God's existence, the agnostics, being the second. In the third group are the atheists who don't believe in God. People who believe in God and know about God but then reject God outright, usually end up in Hell.

God plays a significant part in all of these people's lives, no matter which group they are in, and whether they are aware of this or not.

Book 9 concentrates on what we as humanity need for our earthly lives and for our eventual salvation with God after our death. This is based on some major challenges from God. The greatest challenge from God is a Massive discerned Inspired Message from God.

It comes from the concept of the Incarnate God being an Incredible Leader for everyone.

Bryan has a variety of books that illuminate his many varied experiences of being with God.

This book, **Before Heaven: Hints Tips Stories,** *builds on Bryan's previous body of work. Pray, think about, and enjoy his new offering.*

*Before **Heaven**: Hints Tips Stories*
Bryan Foster

Preface

Most points in this Book 9, 2023, have come from God to the author, and I would suggest, to others worldwide, whenever God so chose to do this. (This is something incredible for all those concerned in various ways about Revelations to humanity from God., whether being the receiver or follower of the receiver, or those impacted by the Revelations, etc..) Many came as direct Revelations (R), most at a specific moment over the past eight years, as well at other times historically. Or as discerned Inspired Messages (IM) over decades from God. Others, no doubt worldwide, are receiving similar information from God, to spread throughout our whole world. I am so pleased that I hopefully will be able to assist others through these many challenges from God.

God's True Unchallengeable Absolute Truths.

Unlike most social media platforms and worldly views of today -

God's divine points, His shared Revelations in *Before Heaven book* are not open to debate, as each one is the direct Truth given by God and is not negotiable. Plus, we can't put God to the Test!

As such, these need to be seen as ABSOLUTE FACTS and not open for discussion on being the Truth.

But, yes, these are open legitimately for **analysis, education, and clarification**, etc.

As with everything from God, no one is <u>forced</u> to believe anything from Him. We are to use our own Free Will and Informed Conscience, which shows God's Absolute Love

in action. Absolute Love gives us absolute freedom. However, we all have the genuine right to believe or not believe, various teachings, readings, or statements, etc. from God. Absolute Love = Absolute choice of options for all individuals within our communities.

Informed Conscience

Yet, we need to have done whatever is needed to understand God's teachings, possibly through various religions, scriptures, beliefs, and reflections, etc. Then pray to God until you feel fully informed about your views or beliefs. This praying could be relatively short in time or sometimes well over months. Then decide what your belief is and feel that it is fully correct and at peace for you in God's eyes, and strongly believe that you won't change your view anytime soon.

These may sometimes appear as being too strongly against those using social media. It will be claimed to be against their free will, free speech, and free religious choices. Is this so though? Any incorrect statements by social media are just that, incorrect. God's Truth is the Truth when we are advised of this Truth by God. (Rs) and (IMs) form this group of Truths. That's life when God is directly involved and not just on a sideline. To be true to the massive divine existence of the ONE God of all time, we can't play a game!!! Yes, we have Free Will for free choices. And an Informed Conscience for our moral and ethical choices. But when God states the Truth at any level He so chooses, we either accept these or rebuke these. The rebuttal is acceptable unless you totally reject God, after knowing God and His Love, Teachings, and Forgiveness. If done as a rejection of their known God, this is evil and is leading toward Hell. *This book states very clearly that the road to somewhere unique, divine, and absolutely loving – for us all – exists if we so choose God and Heaven and not Evil and Hell.*

Hell is for those who totally reject God at death, after knowing of and about God, on Earth, 'Before Heaven'. Hence, God is real, understood, and known about in detail, but is then rejected by evil people.

The key moments are just before and after death!!! A final Rejection of the understood God of Absolute Love after death = Hell!!!

Clarity of God's Truths is Essential.

This book is written for all people who seriously desire to live with God in Heaven, after their time on Earth. Or live on any other divine celestial body (if any) with other living creations from God, as chosen by God! So many of us have very little idea how we go about this. Our world, especially the Western first world, is seriously challenged by the massive distractions thrown at us *Before Heaven* from all corners of the world. In recent times many of us have lost much of our real and authentic loving lifestyles, that were the reality a few decades ago. It was the shared domain of our Absolutely Loving God and us. This especially involves the world's diminishing Love of the One and Only Creator of everything within our world and in our whole human community.

*Before **Heaven**: Hints Tips Stories*
Bryan Foster

Special Stories from God and Author

Book 9 in the *'GOD Today' Series,* highlights being with God throughout our lives. The author is living and experiencing God, God's Revelations, and Inspired Divine Messages, substantially throughout his life. You, the reader, are also now part of this lived experience of God today. **Special articles in this Book 9 contain some of the most extraordinary Revelations, Inspired Messages, and signs from God for all of today's people worldwide, no matter their religion and beliefs in God, culture, life, and death experiences.** The articles shared throughout Book 9, are both from God and from the author, with God included mostly in these stories. God's stories have been around since the start of time, right up until today. Mine have been around for upwards of 60 years. God, my wife Karen, and I, became a 'team' over the decades. *I grew closer and closer to God as my life evolved, as did Karen. We are all individually invited to do the same to the best of our abilities; hopefully with various opportunities for assistance, as needed.* **You too are very much invited to join us, along with all others searching for, and living, God Today. Make a supportive God Team, follow God, and find your own special PEACE.**

The stories from God... *are a set from the divine level, while another set is from my human level and experiences, mostly with God.* I will hopefully interest many people *Before **Heaven*** to search for and eventually discover God in their lives, through their own experiences, along with similar experiences of others. Or to bring God a lot closer to themselves as each person grows in

*Before **Heaven**: Hints Tips Stories*
Bryan Foster

Wisdom, openness, and eagerness to become one with our One and Only God of all time, for all religions and all people.

We all love stories, and when these are about God or us, each should take on a special significance. This book, *Before Heaven: Hints Tips Stories,* contains stories we should all relate to or become engaged with over time. Each one should help bring each of us closer to God and various members of humanity. We need to see God more and to legitimately help and see various other people impacted in almost everything we do.

God is always present and waiting to be called upon positively. We need to take up that challenge often.
God is Absolute Love, Perfectly Good, and Perfectly Just.
Fully and Absolutely Forgiving of those truly sorry for their sins.

Everything about God is Loving beyond our human comprehension!!!

We each need to accept God's offering to us of Absolute Love!!!

And to move as closely as possible to God throughout our lives.
God is the Complete Answer for our Salvation.
God Absolutely wants us to be with Him in Heaven!

With God - That is our final choice and option at death – God/Heaven or Hell!

Before **Heaven**: *Hints Tips Stories*
Bryan Foster

Something quite strange and different occurred to me in December last year. I had almost finished this book's draft and edit and was preparing to publish it when God sent me a special message.

Titled #A by me. This was followed by another special message in January this year. I Titled it #B - Only One Religion for All People Worldwide and Forever. The world needs to Transition to this reality ASAP.

#A is Phenomenal, Unique, and Spectacular! The challenge is that it is 'soooo" Massive and 'soooo' Important, that it needs to at least be mentioned seriously, whether it is the full Truth or not!

Is it a Revelation? An Inspired Message from God? Or neither? It wasn't received as my previous ones were received. It was presented to me differently. I am still trying to appreciate it as a Revelation or a discerned Inspired Message or something else.

It could even end up being nothing of any real importance, but I do doubt this statement. These introductory points will be explained and developed in this Book 9. I will hopefully be helping the reader appreciate where I am going with this, and the decisions being made along the way.

I hope each reader and various people impacted by these discussion points, will become closer to God and more at One with God, Religion, Heaven, God's Absolute Love, and God's Forgiveness, etc.

*Before **Heaven**: Hints Tips Stories*
Bryan Foster

Introduction

Before Heaven: Hints Tips Stories, *2023*, continues to search for the answers and is working towards bringing us all closer to our God and other people worldwide. Various theologies and scholarly teachings from God and others, ask us many genuine and necessary questions about the teachings and commandments, etc. from God.

Following are the seven highlighted themes we need to seriously consider at this stage *Before Heaven*, as we work our way towards our salvation with God at our deaths. Book 10 concludes this Series with a further set of highlighted themes from God. God has strongly advised the author to emphasise that He Needs us all to be Saved with Him in Heaven. The onus is on all humanity to do the right things, including not sinning, i.e., turning away from God, especially seriously, to loving our God Absolutely. And for sinners to seek deep Love and Forgiveness from those who have seriously sinned against God and others worldwide.

The seven key topics in Book 9 are:

1. Physical Evidence of God

> Author's 21+1 Revelations from God (1982, 2016, 2018)
>
> Tears from God
>
> Unique Photographic sun, cloud, rainbow, Images, etc. from God
>
> Coincidences and God

2. 1 God Only Forever for All People and All Religions

Before **Heaven**: *Hints Tips Stories*
Bryan Foster

3. Humans, Plants, Animals, and probably, inert objects, can go to Heaven – still a mystery from God for us to understand these options

4. Medical Issues – a possible starting point to assist individuals to compare health issues with each other, as we all have medical issues whose impact, we can learn from each other. How to support each other. Etc.

5. Hell: God Aware, and Informed peoples' Rejection of God, probably sees these people go to Hell at death!

6. Jesus and Mahomad – Two Incarnations of God

7. ******** The MASSIVE and SPECTACULAR Question for All******** – 4 billion incarnations??? Massive, Unique, Incarnations of half the earth's population. And the other half is led by these Incarnated people. Introduction, Exploration, and Possible Answers are Discussed in this Book 9, and continue to Book 10 to see the author's appreciation and understanding at that point in time. This is so that I can publish the latest teaching from God, not where we are now, but where the teaching will be nearest the day of publication.

The general approach of this book begins with an invitation for all people to be open to God and for others who follow God closely or who want to be so much closer to God and each other person worldwide, to make the necessary approaches to gain a closeness, which should help others also to feel and be close to our most Loving God of eternity. This should lead to a life of Love, Forgiveness, Happiness, and Joy.

As humanity continues to discover how the spiritual, religious, and physical worlds approach the important aspects of life and people more than ever, the need for God and God's teachings, ethics, commandments, etc., begin to become so necessary for

*Before **Heaven**: Hints Tips Stories*
Bryan Foster

us all, that we may hopefully be able to find God in our lives and help to make God number 1 and essential for us all, so as to become one with God and all of humanity, on our way to being saved with God, at Home in Heaven, ideally.

Book 9 helps to show us the best way to bring each of us closer to God and to our Absolute positive destination at death, Heaven. It also warns us of the other major eventuality for evil people who know God but rejects God outright, at death, which is probably Hell.

We have such incredible power leading us to what God very much wants for us all, Heaven, at our deaths. For the great majority of people, this will eventually be with our Absolutely Loving God. For what appears to be quite a minimum of people, very unfortunately they will, at their deaths, be sent or will self-select to end up in Hell, an existence of total isolation and hate. Self-selections occur when evil people freely choose evil and hell at death. Because they see this as ideal, after being seriously evil within their *'before Heaven'* lives.

It was this #7 highlighted theme, from these just listed themes on the previous page, and on this page, where I was challenged by God when I awoke at 3am one night this year. Interestingly, this waking time of 3am, also occurred on both nights when the 21 Revelations were shared with me in 2016 (15) and 2018 (6). Yet, this time it seems to be different! No instruction to write down exactly what God said to me, nor any details on it being an (IM) over time. I have been considering this for almost a year – that shows the strong possibility and level of this message from God.

*Before **Heaven**: Hints Tips Stories*
Bryan Foster

At this editing stage, I will now adjust the discussions on this incredibly different but interesting statement from God explored in this book, to reflect God's latest input.

Many of the themes covered in this Book 9, *Before Heaven: Hints Tips Stories*, are quite difficult to present and explain overall. One is a Massive God Theme and requires quite an amount of intellectual and reflective consideration. It is very much from God. But it also may not be what it was first considered as, a Revelation. Books 9 and 10 will both develop the appreciation of God's teachings and levels received from God, of the 2022 message from God, and of the books 1-8, before the *Before Heaven* books. Book 9 introduces so much that is from God and for us to appreciate at higher levels than expected. There are various challenges for us all to understand and then consider how best to advise others within our world, especially for those searching for God's special place and special impact on today's people within today's world, no matter their religion, their beliefs in One God Only, their Love of the Absolute God of Love, etc.

Something extremely pressing and necessary for our world today, and open to so much Love, has been developing from God within me, and no doubt many other believers, for decades now. A most spectacular part of this growth and development is the closeness to God many of us have been experiencing at a higher level than we would have ever expected. This is also possible for so many people today. God has both challenged and rewarded us along the way, to discover the divinity of God and our own place within God's calling for believers within our world. Within different religions and cultures, we all need to act seriously according to God's Need of us all i.e., to eventually grow to the belief in Only One God and Only One Religion,

*Before **Heaven**: Hints Tips Stories*
Bryan Foster

God Loving all People Equally, as part of all creation within our One God world of today and the whole future of the world.

I am now personally living the most enjoyable and Loving aspect of my life. I would also joyfully add my wife, Karen, to this same or similar stage. Developing our relationships with God, and as much of creation as possible has certainly depthed both of our experiences with the One and Only God of eternity and the various communities we experience or live within over the decades. We have learned to search for the divine God in everything, except evil.

Books 9 and 10 will bring most of the key points, Revelations, and discerned, divine, Inspired Messages, together as One, being a large group of *'Hints Tips Stories'* of many of our experiences with God and various worldly groups already close to God or developing as such. These also concentrate on the Hints, Tips, and Stories for Us All. These developed along a most interesting pathway over my whole life, from 10 years of age when I started being an altar boy in my local church. 55 years later and God is my absolute mainstay and offers us, Absolute Love, forever. I believe that I place God as #1 for everything. Karen lives life this way too – God is always her #1! The more this occurs, the greater and the more powerful God becomes for Karen and me, and we for each other. Along with all those we engage with, often live as closely as possible to a similar, divine, Godly lifestyle.

For me, the most powerful, inspirational, and often unique ways, come directly from God, God Incarnates, Angels, Prophets, Holy people, Intelligent and Highly Educated people, and Genuine Authentic people of all persuasions who are living, working, and praying to be closer to God and each other, each day of their lives.

Extremely fortunate for me and for those before me, and those following me, God has revealed various Revelations for sharing with the world. The most common ones explored and discussed throughout this *'God Today' Series*, were revealed to me in 1982, 2016, and 2018. Next, we have two others just received from 2022 and 2023. There is a rather challenging approach needed to clarify, what level these last two are? Revelation, Inspired Message, or Neither? The doubt exists due to how each was received from God, and the actual truthfulness of each? Both will be explored and analysed in detail over time. It is almost certain that this will take more time than the publication of this book really allows. It will, more than likely, continue after Book 9's publication. If so, further exploration will occur down the line.

The latest two messages from God, 2022 and 2023, were subsequently analysed by me in an initial basic fashion, to gain a brief, authentic, appreciation of what God has given me, and most likely given to many others worldwide. You would imagine that people who received these possible Revelations from God would be given similar instructions to share these Revelations/Inspired Messages worldwide across all genuine religions and communities. **It is then that a fuller appreciation, analysis, evaluation, and shared beliefs, will start to become the basis for the One and Only God, One Religion Only, for all People, for all of Eternity.** This is a key requirement from God, which I received from God through His Informed Messages (IM) to me and to our religions and communities.

*Before **Heaven**: Hints Tips Stories*
Bryan Foster

Along similar lines, I have received numerous Inspired Messages from God over many decades, which I have discerned or am still discerning, and then passing these on to worldwide communities – various religions, cultures, eras, nationalities, etc. These books 9 and 10 include 100+ Inspired Messages and Revelations (Truths) from God and the (IM) Inspired Messages were discerned as the Truth from God over many years, and in some cases, over decades. This book, in the 10 books *'God Today' Series*, includes some very interesting and challenging approaches to humankind from God. Some of these include to me (shared with the readers throughout): Revelations 21+1, 1982, 2016, 2018, and Inspired Messages 100+ from God; the genuine Images most UNIQUELY involving the sun, clouds, moon e.g., giant 'Easter Sun Cross' and Sun Arrows and Flares, etc. (See Book 4 for many UNIQUE photographic images from God. See also three example images in this Book 9).; 'Tears from God' for us to prove something from God to us as being correct and divine; and a highly possible request for the author to be a prophet for God.

Just after completing the writing and during the final editing of this book, **God sent a Massive and Final Revelation or (IM), or something else, or 'possibly nothing'**, for today's world. **If this is so major and mind-blowing, that its explanations and necessary details are included in an introductory degree, then much scholarship is needed overall. Various points for consideration are discussed towards the end of this book.**

I imagine that God will need to tell us more for an accurate assessment of this one Revelation or Inspired Message, or even if it is something else from God? It is so much of a challenge, particularly due to its Massiveness, Powerfulness, and total

Before **Heaven**: *Hints Tips Stories*
Bryan Foster

Loving, Openness of God for us all. **God said to me, that He wants all humans to Go Home to Him in Heaven. This is so much up to each of us individually before Heaven and at death.**

This latest Revelation, Inspired Message, or whatever else it could be, assists incredibly strongly with this authentic, divine, Godly aim!

This last message for this book encourages us strongly to move towards God throughout our lives, so as to become One with the One and Only God in Heaven!

Twice over the past few years, three times when including God's information to me one recent night at 3am. God has awoken me, while I was caravan/trailer camping on the plains and at the foot of the nearby Mt Warning/Wollumbin in the northern rivers of New South Wales, Australia. As a most beautiful, former volcano's volcanic core, it remains and is seen from long distances away in all directions. Captain Cook, who discovered Australia for England, named it Mt Warning due to the roughness at sea off its coast in northern New South Wales.

I will be considering the recent teachings from God about the 4 billion God Incarnates message sent in December, 2022. Even though it seemed quite strongly accurate when suggested as God spoke to me that December. God has now informed me that this incredibly powerful and inspirational teaching for all people, needs considerable scholarship and leadership from scriptural and religious experts worldwide. **We need to wait and**

see how the details develop before any implementation, if any. But also, being prepared to act quickly if #A is the Truth from God.

Why mightn't this Massive and Powerful message be a real Revelation or discerned Inspired Message from God? The standard approach by God for each one was not expressed or used when He was revealing it. There was no direction to transcribe whatever it was that God was sending, for it to be a Revelation. Nor was there any long period of time. It could be decades in some circumstances, when it was considered seriously, studied intimately, reflected upon, and discussed with various religiously informed people, along with academics and scholars within this area of expertise until a decision hopefully will be reached for it to be an Inspired Message, if not a Revelation, or nothing at all?

True, the first Revelation to me was received in 1982 during a praying over me by a charismatic school principal at the first secondary school I was to teach in and on the school's 'Commitment to God' day. Coincidently, it was my 25th birthday and my resignation from this school. It was the day when my family and I moved houses to a small country town, Tara, where I began my first principalship in a primary school. This is another way I believe God passes Revelations to people, i.e., through coincidences. Therefore, I believe the process to see this as a massive teaching from God, is yet to come.

This has been a most enjoyable, yet challenging book to write. So many special God and humanity themes, all helping us with our journey Home to Heaven with God. Included are various Revelations and Inspired Messages from God for us all. The Massive Message I received in December last year, after the

*Before **Heaven**: Hints Tips Stories*
Bryan Foster

book had been written and edited, added so much to this publication. But it wasn't all plain sailing. December's Message may have been on any level, due to the way God presented it to me. I am still reflecting, praying, and discussing it, so as to help with a decision as soon as possible.

Before **Heaven**: *Hints Tips Stories*
Bryan Foster

Highlighted Themes Explored

1. God is no unimaginable existence. God is the existence of Absolute Love and Forgiveness, plus, plus, plus. His desire for each person, along with all His living creations, is **to end up with God at Home in Heaven at our deaths**. Several physical examples help us all appreciate and understand God's existence as explained and highlighted in this Book 9. The **photographic images from God** to the author, (see Book 4 for new unique images never seen before by the author and most others) are mostly formed from the sun, moon, and clouds, which come from God to assist us all, and also challenge us in deeply spiritual ways, to exist with God in today's world, in a one-on-one existence. **Tears from God** are also examples of the physical evidence of God. These come to people who are very close to God and show God's support and encouragement to do what God needs of us. **'Coincidence'** is also quite necessary for God. Meeting my wife to be at a Catholic teachers' college, was not initially destined to occur. But it did. I was enrolled in a science degree at a new university in Brisbane, and Karen was applying for a teachers'/librarian course at the ANU in Canberra. I changed my mind for quite odd reasons, after accepting the science degree. Karen also changed her mind and chose teaching, at the same teachers' college as I had chosen. No links between us existed until meeting at college. We truly believe that God played a major role in our meeting and marrying - three years later. (More details earlier in this Series.) My **receiving the 21+1 Revelations directly from** God is also physical evidence from God.

2. Knowing that there is **Only One God for all Eternity, for all people, all religions, and all cultures,** highlights how we

need to think and live our lives, our aims, and our relationships with all the people we encounter, so as to live the best lives we can. This means so much for how we then decide on our best lifestyles so as to lead each of us to the best outcomes we can when we die.

For most people, the concept of Heaven, Hell, and the end of our lives, leads us to a quite meaningful and necessary existence for each of us to decide how we will end up, along with God's input and decisions. Both God and we have serious decisions to make when we die. Absolute love with God and humanity leads to Heaven, while absolute hate and evil lead to Hell. People who know and understand God and God's reality and teachings, etc. but who then reject God outright, are evil and their end lives are almost certainly directed to Hell.

3. Heaven has always seemed to have been for the absolute love of God and each human who ended up with God in Heaven. However, this is not the full story. People are not the only ones who can qualify to share God's and humanity's absolute loving existence. **All of God's living creations have an incredible opportunity to end up with each other with God in Heaven**. This place is for all humans, fauna, and flora, and probably all inert (not living or ever alive) **God-created objects** too. How and why, this happens is still a mystery from God to us. No doubt there is still the aspect of God's Absolute Love, this time for all His living creations, in addition to all of humanity.

4. **Medical issues** have been introduced for consideration for us to consider various medical comparisons, reactions, and end results each of these may have on us, if these are applicably so. Why medical stories? Health professionals and Medicine affects all of us at various levels and in various ways. Because all life

forms develop similarly, medical intervention is one such way in which we may all be able to take evasive or positive steps in various directions to help us heal or be affected in positive ways. **Having like-with-like experiences, or similar-with-similar ones, allows for such comparisons to be considered real and true.** Through these comparisons, we should not only be able to develop stronger relationships with those like us, but also to develop plans for solutions for various difficulties and challenges we may have with God and others with whom we are in contact.

5. **Hell and evil** are two of those topics people are not too keen on discussing. This is often out of personal ignorance of what each topic means, or the possible outcomes which may eventuate, or along with a sometimes-inherent fear and desire not to become involved in the unknown or the evil that is in its existence. A bit of, hiding from the 'baddie' maybe? Fear usually permeates the reality of evil and Hell. And so, it should, because **people can end up existing in this evil, hell domain for eternity. In total isolation, totally surrounded by evil, fear, and the perennial destruction of themselves forever, and all that time being by themselves and totally isolated individually.**

6. Interestingly, this next topic combines beliefs and very high 'Wow' factors for all people considering such key topics and end results for us and many others worldwide. Two Incarnations have been highlighted by God in the fifteen Revelations He sent me in May 2016, while I was camping on the planes of Mt Warning/Wollumbin on the Northern Rivers of New South Wales, Australia. Most people would agree that Jesus Christ was both fully man and fully God. **Revelation #15 from God in 2016, stated that both Jesus and *Mahomad**

(Muhammad) were God Incarnate, each being fully God and fully Human. Such a concept is obviously sheer brilliance from a most Absolutely Loving God. Life is about the absolute love of God and each other. Two most incredible examples of such unique and necessary Incarnations, Jesus and Mahomad, show us in the most extraordinary ways, how to aim to be genuinely one with God and each other. Now that's a most incredible sign of support from God and each of us.

7. Once we **understand and appreciate what God's Incarnations are** and what they can possibly do, we can start to explore how these may be formed and what each of these Incarnations can do. Secondly, once we appreciate that **Jesus was the first one and that *Mahomad was the second example known to us of the Incarnations introduced to us by God as God's #15 Revelation in 2016** to the author, the greater will be our Love of God and of God's creations. To then be open to other Incarnations of God to us, will be something well beyond our normal worldly endeavours. Probably it will be Divine and Godly.

Incarnations are Divine (fully God) and Physical (fully human). Why would there be only two Incarnations throughout all of eternity, and in only one small geographical region on Earth? This is especially as God can do anything! Anywhere and Anything for any reason - with whomever or whatever He chooses! But always out of absolute Love for all of creation.

Hence, if God wanted to assist all His creations, then so be it!!! He will! This now brings to the fore something about Absolute Love from an Absolutely Loving and Forgiving God. Something which will directly help all of creation. **Help all** people to be figuratively, but yet, totally real, led, carried, and assisted by God forever. For this to occur there will be a possible need to have Incarnated people throughout the world. Each Incarnated person would have the responsibility to assist various humans individually at various times throughout their lives. Will this occur? Only time will tell! But it is always a genuine possibility for God to set in action.

If this statement from God is eventually seen to be true, what absolutely, mind-boggling and exceptionally generous Absolute Love from God, the One and Only God of eternity. Imagine being guided and directed by God for every second of your life – in this case through an Incarnated God, One fully God with a fully modern human. To top this off in a way nobody would have ever surely imagined, of which the author is aware, God may link each person on earth to an incarnated God chosen by Him from humanity. If this is authentically so, then each Incarnated God/person on earth is a personal divine guide, fully God and fully Human, for each human person living on Earth. On today's count, there are then 4 billion humans and 4 billion God-incarnated people. Overall, 4 billion people and 4 billion Incarnated people on Earth. Imagine the Absolute Love emanating throughout the world now or in those days in the future. It would be so Heavenly and authentically Absolute Love and Forgiveness.

Yes, we all still must make our own informed decisions, but God will then be so close, as to be the ultimate guide to Good and God Himself, and the Absolutely Loving God!!! God wants all His creations to be One with Him in Heaven at all our deaths – Humans, Flora, and Fauna. Also probably includes the inert creations of God.

Before **Heaven**: *Hints Tips Stories*
Bryan Foster

Author - Overview

Karen Foster and I have been married for forty-five years this year. We have three adult children and four grandchildren. Our two eldest adult children Leigh-Maree and Andrew are teachers, while our third, Jacqui, has just completed her science degree with first-class honours at the University of Queensland.

These days I concentrate on my book writings, having permanently retired from the teaching of religion after 42 years. The main *Series* now is the *'GOD Today' Series* of ten books/photobooks, which began being compiled in 2016 and concluded in 2023 - eight full years of recording God's Revelations, discerning Inspired Messages (over decades at times) and Unique Sun Images for people everywhere. The *Series* includes nonfiction books, photobooks, videos, websites, and social networking platforms.

I taught thirty years of 'Study of Religion' to years/grades 11 and 12; been a primary/elementary school principal, twice; and an assistant principal for religious education/pastoral care/administration in secondary/high school for (12 years). I believe that I played a considerable role in religious schools, parishes, and the Church deanery. Have been a president and secretary of both parish and deanery pastoral councils. As well as president of my children's primary school's Parents and Friends Association, twice.

Author's Credibility

I have been receiving Revelations since 1982 and divine Inspired Messages from God for decades since my mid-teenage years. The (IMs) seem to have most often come on the back of my religious studies and consequent religious, education, theological, and Religious Education qualifications over more than 10 years. My leadership positions within Catholic schools and the local parishes and deanery, support the place of leadership within the Church. 42 years of leadership and teaching within Catholic schools, set me up for substantial positioning within the education and religious wings of the Catholic Church. The published, and yet-to-be-published books (2023), play a major part in my influence worldwide. 10 books make up this contemporary *'God Today' Series*, along with photobooks, textbooks, websites, videos, etc.

To assist with credibility, I have included several reasons why these are the Truth from God to be heard across our world. There are explanations for the reader throughout to support the many Revelations (R) and discerned Inspired Messages (IM) from God. Readers of previous books in this *'God Today' Series* will notice the depth and variety of these challenging Revelations from God, as explained in this latest book. **These last two books are bringing together significant topics and themes of importance, for the reader from God, along with a couple of extra special (R)s or (IM)s.**

This should be a very special *Series* for us all. What more could we want than to bring God's Revelations, and discerned Inspired Messages together in one *Series*? To live God's life expectations of us all. To become a strong part of God's Absolute Love for all of creation.

1God.world: One God for All (2016) and *Where's God? Revelations Today* (2018) and *Where's God? Revelations Today Photobook Companion: GOD's Signs* (2018) invited us to join in discovering God, God's Revelations (R), and God's discerned Inspired Messages (IM), as we strive to find our own personal and communal salvation with God. Being aware of coincidences and signs from God to people, notably including us, helps our journey to God and Heaven.

We should also discover that God works in many ways, often being quite up-front to us all, through the challenges He sets us throughout our lives. The absolute Truth from God, as found in the decisions we make on various issues, teachings, and commandments, enhances our own lives and the Truth we accept from God, often after searching the evidence and signs from God of the Truth.

#A revealed by God to me in Dec. 2022, is going to be worked on continually by me, and hopefully, by others who are scholars, theologians, religious leaders, etc. of various religions worldwide, until a decision can be made. The two largest religions in the world, Catholicism and Islam, along with other interested worldwide religions can assist. I will include what I do to assist with a solution to this dilemma in the next book, Book 10. My major purpose, as instructed by God, is to write and publish Books and other publications worldwide.

One God. One Religion.

There now needs to be times when people and religious leaders, theologians, scriptural scholars, and various other key people within each genuine religion, can start developing a more acceptable **Single Religion** with the **One and Only God of Eternity, as per God's teachings, especially in this '*God Today' Series.***

Before **Heaven**: *Hints Tips Stories*
Bryan Foster

This is just as, "One God only – One God," from God challenged us in Book 1 of this series – *1 God.world: One God for All*, (2016). **Each religion's leaders, scholars, and various key members of all genuine religions need to challenge their separation from each other.** It was explained in Book 1 - *1God.world: One God of All,* **that all genuine and authentic religions need to combine with each other. To accept that there is Only One Religion for all time, for all people and all cultures, and One God Only forever, past, present, and future.**

This is the absolute basis of existence. Everything coming from, and going to, our One and Only God of eternity. **It is time, revealed God**! Be very open to what God has to offer each one of us uniquely. We are all equal. We are all loved equally in 'God's eyes'. *We need to develop as just One Religion for humanity. Each genuine religion needs to highlight that there should be Only One God, religion, set of beliefs, etc.*

Christianity, Islam, Hinduism, and Judaism on there being only 1 God for us all!

There is a basic similarity about the existence of 1 God between the mainline religions of the world. These religions represent about 70% of the world's population. An external observer could quite legitimately believe that these religions are referring to the same God.

However, the doctrine of each religion would not accept the others' God as their own - even though each believes in just 1 God. Christianity and Judaism believe in the same God, but

Judaism does not believe in the Trinity of Christianity. *1God.world: One God for All* is an explanation of personal discovery and discernment over 55 years. This discernment has come from academic studies, a personal and communal religious life, wide reading and discussions, religious teaching vocation/career, and many prayerful interactions with God.

An appreciation of each religion's doctrine of God has been a part of the discovery. From these discoveries came the discerned realisation that each religion follows the One same God.

Each of these religions believes in 1 God, teaches about 1 God, has similar moral and ethical beliefs about God, and from an outsider's perspective, each is apparently engaging with the same God. From my discernment over decades and prayerful encounters with God, I must believe in the one true God being the same God for all people. That there is only 1 God.

So much of this can be observed from each religion's scriptural sources and contemporary commentary; some examples follow.

Hinduism emphasises One God, Brahman, who has many manifestations. Judaism has Yahweh as the Only God and entity to be praised - there are no other gods. Christianity has One God. The Trinity is the One God but with three 'persons' in one. Islam has One God. Islam rejects all other claimed gods. Islam teaches about the same God as Christianity and Judaism but believes God is revealed imperfectly in these religions. Each religion developed at a particular time and place in history. God revealed Godself to each religious community, which then developed accordingly.

Some key scriptural quotes from each religion's main sources show the views of the four mainline world religions on God. This is an overview and in no way meant to be a concise explanation. Note, that in each quote there is only 1 God mentioned.

Hinduism: "He is One only without a second." (Chandogya Upanishad 6:2:1) "O friends do not worship anybody but Him, the Divine One. Praise Him alone." (Rigveda 8:1:1) "Brahman is all… He who concentrates on Brahman in all his actions shall surely reach Brahman." (Bhagavad Gita IV:12:24)

Islam: "He is the One God; the Creator, the Initiator, the Designer… (Qur'an 59:24) Say, "He is God, the One. God, to Whom the creatures turn for their needs. He begets not, nor was He begotten, and there is none like Him." (Qur'an, 112:1-4)
"God, there is no God but Him, The Living, the Eternal One." (Qur'an 2:225)

Judaism (and Christianity):

"Hear, O Israel: The LORD is our God, the LORD alone. You shall love the LORD your God with all your heart, and with all your soul, and with all your might." (Deuteronomy 6:4-5) "…so that they may know, from the rising of the sun and from the west, that there is no one besides me; I am the LORD, and there is no other..." (Isiah 45:6)

"Know therefore that the LORD your God is God, the faithful God who maintains covenant loyalty with those who love him and keep his commandments, to a thousand generations..." (Deuteronomy 7:9)

Christianity: "Jesus answered, 'The First is, 'Hear oh Israel: the Lord our God, the Lord is one...'" (Mark 12:29)

"Jesus answered him, 'It is written, Worship the Lord your God, and serve only him.'" (Luke 4:8)

"He said to him, 'What is written in the law? What do you read there?' He answered, 'You shall love the Lord your God with all your heart, and with all your soul, and with all your strength, and with all your mind; and your neighbour as yourself.'" (Luke 10:27)

God – Revelations (R) and discerned Inspired Messages (IM) to the Author www.islam-gu www.irf.net/Hinduism www.hindudharmaforums.com
NRSV, www.biblegateway.com

Commentators' Views on 1 God Only Forever

Let us consider what commentators have to say about who God is for each of the four largest world religions. Once again it is worth noting how so much from each religion points to 1 God only. Even though each religion believes in their own God as the God as seen from the commentators mentioned, it is believed that a normal outside observer should be able to claim that each religion is referring to the same God. That there is 'One God for All' humanity. Also, note how various commentators are virtually stating this belief, yet with some resistance.

Hinduism believes in one God, Brahman, who is manifested in many other Gods. This belief in one supreme God is supported by many commentators of this religion. (Archer, P., 2014, BBC, Himalayan Academy) Peta Goldburg emphasises that Brahman is above all the gods and is not a god but is the one from whom the gods derive their power. (2009) 'Godweb' when discussing Brahman notes the considerable similarity between the characteristics attributed to Brahman as the supreme God and the monotheistic God of Christianity, Islam, and Judaism.

Islam believes in Allah being the one true God as taught by Muhammad and professed in the Shahadah: 'There is no God but God and Muhammad is God's messenger'. (Aslan, R., 2012) The specific God, Allah, is the one and only God who controls everything. (Goldburg, P., 2009; Archer, P., 2014) There is an emphasis on only worshipping God and nothing else. (Why Islam; Islam Guide). The imperfection of God in the other monotheistic religions of Christianity and Judaism is emphasised. (Religion Facts) 'Why Islam' challenges standard Islamic belief and goes further by noting that this is God for all of humanity, not any specific race or tribe of people.

One of Christianity's overarching Church documents is from the Catechism of the Catholic Church. It emphasises one God only. This is also the first line in the Apostle's Creed prayer. The Catechism emphasises that the one God teaching has its roots in both the Old Testament (also of the Jews) and the New Testament. (Vatican) An ultimate source is emphasised in Thomas Aquinas' 'Five Ways' and is seen as the one God. (Hemler, I., 2014) Interestingly, Ian Elmer in a Redemptorist's publication highlights that no religion, denomination, or Church has an absolute claim on God. He states that Christians should claim that God became human and can be found in a church, synagogue, mosque, temple, family, or nature. He then seems to place some doubt on this encompassing statement by noting that it is only through the Catholic Eucharist that any presence of God is possible. Judaism has a belief in one God, which has been recorded throughout their many thousands of years. (Goldburg, P., 2009) The first five principles stated in the religion's 'Thirteen Principles of Faith' highlight the one God and the unique characteristics of that God. (Archer, P., 2014) The Shema prayer of Judaism also highlights the one God only. That God is a complete entity, who created the universe and whom we must praise. (Jewfaq) BBC emphasises that all Jews have a personal Covenant relationship with the one God and that God is very much present in this world. (also, MyJewishLearning) This book's website, *www.1God.world*, will have web links to various referenced websites listed.

*Before **Heaven**: Hints Tips Stories*
Bryan Foster

God Asked if I would be One of His Prophets

On the early morning of 29 May 2016, at about 3am, God revealed 15 Revelations to me. Each was written down by me as instructed to do by God. *A 'bombshell' of a statement was also written halfway through receiving the Revelations. It was out of the blue but incredibly powerful. It wasn't until three years later, in 2019, that the content was accepted by me as very important. For some reason. it didn't seem important to me for quite a while.*

It was presented similar to the two lines following and stated that:

I am a prophet

prophets are true.

This statement has remained there in the Revelations' notes from God for almost four years without me realising the implications and reality of it. It was presented differently from the other Revelations. It was separated but still on the bottom of the page and wasn't listed in rows as the other Revelations were.

After much reflection and discernment of what is the Truth, it now places much onus on me to fully accept it and do what is required to promulgate these Revelations to the world, whether as a prophet or not. It all came very apparent on Easter Sunday Eve in 2019 at my home on the Gold Coast, Australia. Tears from God clinched the acceptance of the reality of this Revelation for both Karen and me. It was accepted as a Divine Godly invitation. It was a very humbling and challenging invitation.

Before **Heaven**: *Hints Tips Stories*
Bryan Foster

At this stage, **I haven't felt worthy enough to decide to accept fully, this rare, honourable, and much-needed role in today's world. These Revelations, 21+1 (or +2, if 2022's if the message to me is true?) from God now need to be promulgated worldwide. I believe that this can occur directly from me or as me being a prophet of God.** This is along with others worldwide who, more than likely, also received these Revelations. This promulgation particularly needs to highlight Revelation #15. It was the last Revelation received in May 2016 - *Jesus and *Mahomad are God*. (*Mahomad was how God spelt it, each time, except once.)

For accuracy, the spelling and punctuation are precise as revealed in the Revelations from God. (N.B. The exact words, spelling and grammar from God are given here as Revelations.) Why the variation in minor spelling of *Mahomad? Unknown.

Another six Revelations were sent from God two and a half years later on 3 November 2018. These concentrate on God and our relationship with God. Once again this occurred around 3am while camping closer to Mt Warning.

21 Revelations in total were revealed, while camping on the plains, and at the foot of Mt Warning, during the early morning hours in 2016 and 2018. A previous Revelation occurred when I was prayed over by the college's charismatic principal, Sr Ann, on my 25th birthday, while being a teacher at my first secondary school in 1982. This first Revelation gave me Tears from God, along with an incredible flow of warmth inside my body, starting when Sr Ann's hands touched my head and travelled down to my feet. That afternoon the family travelled to Tara in southern Queensland, to begin my first primary/elementary principalship. Note the coincidences and timings used by God.

Before **Heaven**: *Hints Tips Stories*
Bryan Foster

These impacted significantly and seriously helped me grow so much closer to God. This made His received Revelations to be 21+1 overall. (1982 - 1, 2016 - 15, 2018 - 6)

In general terms, the first 14 Revelations from 2016 are to do with people, their respect and honesty with God and each other; their expected behaviour, and God's messages for a world in need. The next seven are primarily based on God as the ABSOLUTE, DIVINE, ALMIGHTY GOD with power and creativity beyond our imagining. What should be our response to God and God's ABSOLUTE LOVE, and FORGIVENESS equally for us all. God seriously strongly desires us all to be saved and go to Heaven at our deaths. Then it is up to each of us to do what we need to do for God and our fellow community members worldwide.

The next few articles in this book are essential for the reader to obtain the necessary background knowledge and appreciation of specific topics needed to appreciate all 21+1 (or +2/3?) Revelations revealed to the author. The credibility of each is assured through God's sent Tears and other forms of 'proof', which are explained in this Book and others within this *Series*.

Also, my discerned understanding of each Inspired Message from God, and the impact these following articles and writings have on Him, and on His anticipated readers are significant. There are three essential edited extracts from the author's previous books in this *'GOD Today' Series*. Those who have been following the *Series* will probably only need to scan over these to update the necessary concepts and content revealed by God at this discovery stage.

*Before **Heaven**: Hints Tips Stories*
Bryan Foster

These details and revealed Truths from God set the scene for the two Incarnations of God. This Revelation highlights the Incarnation of Jesus and Mahomad being both fully human and fully God. These are also available for any other genuine religion so that each can benefit from this Revelation and others.

Surprisingly, after Book 9 was virtually finished and was being edited, God sent another Divine Message, but it wasn't clear whether it was a Revelation? (I wasn't asked to write it down by God, as for the other Revelations, except one from 1982, and this last one from 2022.) Or whether it was a discerned Inspired Message from God. I, therefore, sat on this one reflecting, researching, etc., for a couple of months and discerned its level of Divine Message by God. It initially felt very strongly to be a Revelation, yet it was given to me in a different way. The more I discerned it, the more it seemed to be an Inspired Message (IM), but it could still be a Revelation (R), or maybe a key divine message? Especially due to its depth and very high importance, and the fact that God can do anything out of Absolute Love that he decides.

The importance lies with the need to get this out to as many religious leaders, theologians, scholars, prophets, holy people, etc. *Sharing a most incredible Divine Message, which initially will probably be a major challenge, due to its enormity and being such a unique and spectacular appreciation of God's Absolute Love for each of us equally. As well as it not being decided what level of message from God it is.* (More prophet details later in this text.)

*Before **Heaven**: Hints Tips Stories*
Bryan Foster

Author's Academic Qualifications:

Master of Education (Religious Education) (ACU, Sydney and Brisbane)
Bachelor of Education (ACU, Brisbane)
Graduate Diploma of Religious Education (ACU, Brisbane)
Diploma of Religious Education (IFE, Brisbane)
Diploma of Teaching (McAuley Teachers' College, Brisbane)

ACU – Australian Catholic University (Sydney and Brisbane)
IFE – Institute of Faith (Brisbane)

Choose your friends very wisely!

Be prepared to change friends if they can't support you in this most necessary search and discovery of God by you and humanity.

If friends can't put God first and appreciate yours and their spiritual and religious needs, in your relationship with God and them, what sort of friends are they? Do they encourage you forward to God, or do they remain disinterested in God and directly or indirectly move you back from God?

*Before **Heaven**: Hints Tips Stories*
Bryan Foster

Only 1 God for everyone, forever!

Physical Evidence of God

Before we go too much further, our whole belief in God is essential for going to Heaven after death, as well as living a similar loving life while on Earth before our deaths. This is a starting point, but there are other ways for finding and then believing in God too.

Three key physical points from my direct experiences at various stages within my lifetime are explained in detail:

1. **I have received 21+1 Revelations from God, and possibly more?** This can occur for anyone as God so decides. A special closeness to God would help considerably. Being awoken around 3am on two nights while caravan camping at the foot/plains of Mt Warning/Wollumbin northern NSW, once in 2016, and the other in 2018, and asked by God, through my mind's eye, to write these down accurately and share with the world. (These original handwritten Revelations do exist. See Handwritten Revelation #15.)

2. **I have experienced God physically when receiving the 'Tears from God'** which flow uncontrollably, are not sobbing tears, but are a very special time when God's existence is very close and loving for you. You are often being given some aspect of the truth to share with our world, or maybe just a special time to develop your relationship with God and others of God's creations. As well as **the warmth moving from head to toe after being prayed over by a religious**

charismatic sister and school principal on my 25th birthday at the secondary school I was teaching in, on their 'Commitment to God' day in 1982.

3. The third way, according to other experiences, **is receiving various natural signs through photographs sent to the camera by God e.g., sun, sun arrows, sun flares, a massive Easter sun cross, double rainbows, sunsets, sunrises, and a moon rise. Plus, various coincidences, throughout life. (See Book 4 and my websites, for these unique and unbelievably, spectacular signs sent by God for our world today. Particularly look for the sun-developed sun flares, sun arrows, and sun rays, etc.)**

All these come from genuine Revelations and contact with God, as the primary source of my evidence.

How would people react if I was to challenge them with the question, "It must be difficult for you to accept or reject the genuine Revelations from God, which I share if Revelations are new to you? For many, this is so rare, hence much of a challenge. Or maybe you haven't been with anyone when they were receiving these or after they were received by them? You could very seriously be wondering, are Revelations from God even possible?" And this is a very good question indeed.

As the years have gone on, I am now in my mid-sixties, I'm most often concluding that believers in God, God's Revelations, and God's inspired messages (IM) to various representatives of humanity, in most cases, are very genuine.

Before **Heaven**: Hints Tips Stories
Bryan Foster

It must be considerably difficult for non-believers or rejectors of God to accept their thoughts and beliefs, while observing directly or seeing others being so content and loving and inviting, to justify their own skewed God rejections and beliefs. It must be even more difficult to hear, read or see what God can do with people when you yourself don't believe any of it? The questions must be asked, "Can you be open to receiving or experiencing God when surrounded by believers? Or when you may get an inkling that there is really a God and that God is so close to you, that if you wanted to be open to God, that openness for God should soon come your way?" Give it a GO!!!

The ultimate challenge, I believe we need to offer the non-believers and non-followers of God, is to not lose the opportunity to meet, pray, reflect, etc., with God and see what Absolute Love can do for you and those around you. This can't hurt or harm you, but it can assist you so outrightly. It is part of the maturity of humans, on their way to being one with God, if possible, now on Earth and immediately at that moment of death. It may even often come down to, who are my genuine friends and believers in God? Who will assist me to find what I am missing or am seriously looking for? Non-believers can help by not ridiculing you, but by being open with you to discover God. Genuine friends and colleagues will give you space and support in your search for God and God's requests of you. It is the vindictive ones around you, who will try and give you no chance to find God!

'Tears from God' - Physical Proof from God

Karen, my wife, has also had input into the final presentation, mainly from an editorial perspective but also as a recipient of the Tears from God. These Tears, which we experience mostly, come when God is uniquely present while the author is writing the books, discussing the books together, or for various themes and explanations contained within or about the books. Also, as God can do anything that is Godly/Good, the Tears may come when unexpected, etc. These are explained in this tenth book, as well.

To ignore these Tears from God for any reason is to challenge God.

We must never put God to the test!

Those fortunate to have experienced these Tears know what these mean because this is part of the Revelation process – people receiving these messages or feelings, etc. from God, need to spread God's Word in whatever way the recipients can do in their circumstances.

Tears from God - A.

The Tears from God is one of the primary means of knowing of God's unique presence and occasion of confirming those Revelations or inspired messages.

In 2016 at the foot of Mt Warning in the Murwillumbah Showgrounds, I was awoken around 3am and told by God in my mind's eye to write down precisely as God sent me 'His' Revelations. The early morning encounter with God is explained in detail shortly in the 'Mt Warning…' story. (See Appendix 2.) This supernatural Revelation was confirmed the following morning at a First Communion Mass in the nearby church in which I married Karen forty-four years ago this year – through a Tears from God moment. Once again, two years later, more Revelations occurred at the foot of Mt Warning

*Before **Heaven**: Hints Tips Stories*
Bryan Foster

Rainforest Park caravan park at the foot of the mountain. These are those Revelations numbered sixteen to twenty-one.

There have been some different experiences, often recorded as photographs and featuring the sun, which seem to show God telling a story or offering a particular message. This message may be literal or metaphorical. Often it is God giving a sign of support, or confirmation of that specific inspired message. A point of encouragement for the message's authenticity and the need for it to be shared with others. In my case, the need to accept my place in the scheme of God's plan and to go and do whatever is required to propagate the Revelations or messages from God are also genuine and very much real aspects!

In 2018 there were five quite similar sunlight events to each other, in close time proximity. One occurred at the foot of Mt Warning just after sunrise, another at Texas on the NSW/Queensland border, and a third was at Straddie, North Stradbroke Island, off Moreton Bay, from Brisbane. In contrast, another two occurred at Kingscliff and Cabarita beaches in northern New South Wales, close to Mt Warning, Australia. I believe that these images are part of the overall methods God uses to make points. These are just one method of many though.

Coincidences and signs often point to special moments. In *Where's God? Revelations Today Photobook Companion: GOD Signs (2nd ed)* these are explored along with previously mentioned various sunlight experiences. Many of the images seem so incredible. Some might even wonder if the photos had been enhanced or changed. Not so, except for one minimal necessary adjustment. (The only exception though is the image of Mt Warning with a small cloud atop its peak. The image needed experimentation of light and colour to give the proper authenticity to that photo's sun's rays emanating from the cloud and travelling outwards and upwards.)

The chosen career/vocation choice to teach and to specialise in teaching religion eventuated in forty-two years of teaching religion in religious schools, including teaching the 'Study of Religion' a senior graduation course to senior students in years eleven and twelve for 30 years. Needing, but also strongly desiring, to start each school day and each religion lesson with some communication with God is incredibly empowering. Class prayer and meditation were highly significant for all these years. The academic Study of Religion classes for years eleven and twelve required not just the academic dimension but also the spiritual dimension. This subject needed intimate knowledge and considerable religious experience, if possible, of the various religions of Christianity, Islam, Judaism, Buddhism, Hinduism, and Australian Indigenous Spirituality.

Teaching religion on these multiple levels every working day for such an extended time develops a genuine spiritual relationship with God in itself.

A truly loving relationship with the Divine! Your day is so much God-based. You truly get to appreciate God from each religion's perspectives and beliefs. Combine this with your own daily prayerful and meditative relationship with God, and a teacher of religious faith has something exceptional and unique from which to share professionally, religiously, and spiritually.

Senior leadership positions in schools and parishes help with developing your relationship with God through different experiences. These positions resulted from my personal, and academic background being based on Theology, Scripture, Liturgy, and Religious Education. Also, from experience gained

*Before **Heaven**: Hints Tips Stories*
Bryan Foster

in leadership positions within schools and through the personal spirituality being shared at various levels by students, teachers, parents, the Church, or other religions from our most popular worldwide religion, Christianity.

Each qualification I studied up to a master's degree has considerable levels of religion covered. Whether you are leading a school as a principal or leading the religious aspect of the religious school as an assistant principal for religious education or senior school levels as a Year Level Coordinator or House Coordinator, you should exemplify and live your relationship with God, your faith, and beliefs. You are challenged daily with everyday human aspects of others' relationship with God, religion, the religious school, etc.

Through all this, *your relationship with God grows and strengthens. Daily you become more one with the one and only God of all time. This Godly relationship continually grows through these many and varied experiences in our religious schools and parishes. Senior parish roles result in similar experiences to the religious school but on a parish or deanery level.* A deanery is a geographical grouping of various local parishes. It is led by the leadership priest who is known as a dean. In my roles of Chair or Secretary of the parish or deanery pastoral councils over the years, you as a non-clergy leader, are primarily at the service, of the liturgical and visionary aspects of a church or deanery. You are there to help facilitate the spiritual, religious, and pastoral growth of members of your parish or deanery. You are also there as a laity to help the priest/s. Through experiencing the challenges and best of all the people you deal with through these roles, you cannot help but be strongly influenced by their challenges, successes, and failures in life and their relationships with God and each other. *The influence this has on strengthening your relationship with God is substantial.*

When you have an authentic, prayerful relationship with God, so much of God's truth becomes apparent for those faithful who are open to God's plans, support, wisdom, etc. *The impact is positively life-changing. You so much trust in God. God helps you through good and bad times. You have genuine compassion and empathy for humanity. God is indeed central to your existence.*

The Revelation placing the one and only God as Number One across all genuine religions becomes real and actual. You then naturally aim to love each other as God does. It is through this prayer, meditation, and action for God's lifestyle (as exemplified by Jesus, God Incarnate) that you are more open to God and more prepared to discern God's messages for yourself and others. Discernment of God's Words becomes not just real, but an essential part of your life.

Karen, my wife of forty-four years, this year, is integral to my relationship with God. Karen adds the depth needed to encounter God in these unique ways. She helps me, as I do her, understand and appreciate God's messages and Revelations through her unwavering support and openness to discuss each moment, each experience, and each Tears from God encounters.

Tears from God – B.

My 'Road to Emmaus' experience, my epiphany, and the 'Commitment to God' day on my 25th birthday, highlighted something extraordinary from God. (See Appendix 4)

It became evident to me, that when God wanted me to know something exceptional was coming from God, there would be a passing on of the Tears from God. *These are not God's tears*

Before **Heaven**: *Hints Tips Stories*
Bryan Foster

physically, but these are tears from God spiritually, which I, and no doubt others, experience physically, emotionally, and spiritually.

There is an overwhelming sense of God's love and presence being intimately experienced at that moment. Words cannot describe what is happening, as it is obvious to the recipient that it is on another level beyond the physical. Tears pouring out in free flow. There are no everyday contorted facial expressions or sobbing, as is typically associated with crying. It isn't crying as we know it, but tears are flowing uncontrollably.

Many others also experience these Tears from God. No one religion can claim this existence solely, as it occurs across several religions. This section mainly looks at the place of the tears in Christianity, Islam, and Hinduism.

Just as these Tears overwhelmed me all those years ago, each time God needs me to realise that something extra special is happening, or that differentiation is necessary between the things of this world and the things God wants me to know about or do, or that I need strong support as part of God's plan, God shares the Tears.

Many will say that this is all just emotion and that the tears come because I am emotional about something. Early on, this was my thought too. However, *over time, there has developed a clear appreciation of the difference between normal emotional and physical tears and those Tears from God.* The difference is somewhat difficult to explain, other than to say that the recipient gets this inherent feeling at the same time as the Tears that God is making it known that God is uniquely present at that moment. **It is not just like feeling God's presence but knowing God is present.** Sometimes you almost hear words from God, but you know these are your words being inspired by God. (See Mt Warning Story, Appendix

*Before **Heaven**: Hints Tips Stories*
Bryan Foster

2) Many people would appreciate this from their own prayer life when messages come to them from God. *It is God's inspiration but through your thoughtful and prayerful words.*

These Tears from God became apparent as I went through the development of these ten books. I needed to be continually reminded that the Revelations and inspired messages of the books were correct. In *1God.world: One God for All* it was especially needed for the central premise and Revelation being unconditionally accepted before it was published: *that there is only one God for all religions, peoples, and cultures - forever.*

As well, all the inspired messages within the book up until the Mt Warning Revelation experience had been discerned as correct over several decades, yet reassurance through the Tears from God was still needed before publication. Because these Tears are from God, it is very important that what I state is correct through genuine discernment. Similar support and verification from God were required for the next books: (#2) *Mt Warning God's Revelation: Photobook Companion to '1God.world (2017)'*; (#3) *Where's GOD: Revelations Today (2018); (#4) Love is the Meaning of Life: God's Love (2018), (#5) Jesus and Mahomad are God (2020);* and (#6) *Love is the Meaning of Life: GOD's Love (2021),* and the last few books in this Series of 10 being books #7,8,9,10 being published up to 2023, with the publication of the Revelations and Discerned Inspired Messages contained within.

With the initial planning done in May 2016 for the first book, it was time to get God's final approval. This was a most exciting time for us, because I needed God's final support before publishing my first book in this *'God Today' Series*. I stood with my wife, Karen, in our kitchen one evening and let her know I

*Before **Heaven**: Hints Tips Stories*
Bryan Foster

wasn't sure of the central premise for publication being singled out and emphasised, as I hadn't had any final confirmation message from God. I was concerned that I might have been over-stepping the mark. *At that moment, a rush of tears filled my eyes – Tears from God answered my call! The message from God was palpable - that it was correct and to go ahead - write the first book in this 'God Today Series' and publish it.* And so was born, the first book in a 10-book *Series,* titled: *1God.world: One God for All* by Bryan Foster, 2016.

Since that time, there have been various other occasions when this assurance has been given, especially at Mt Warning, which has now become my place of God. Unfortunately, and with much angst and sorrow, I must advise my readers that it appears, due to a first people's claim on this whole mountain, that we may never get to drive to the park from where the walkers used to begin. And the walkers won't be able to walk the mountain again. It looks like being a very sad result, as so many people won't experience their God or their spirituality on this mountain again. And they will probably never see the places they used to go on the mountain. It was here that many of my authentic and unique images as selfies containing the sun, sun flares, and sun arrows were seen streaming through the gaps in the sparkling rainforest foliage. Most of these unique images are found in Book #4, *Where's God? Revelations Today Photobook Companion: GOD Signs (2nd ed)* (2018). A number of these videos and photos evolved into a video of this topic being recorded with Mt Warning as a background.

**See the 'Tears from God'...' video at https://www.youtube.com/watch?v=z5mmNvIKko4

*Before **Heaven**: Hints Tips Stories*
Bryan Foster

I realise many people will challenge my disappointment in this. However, all I can say is that I inherently know it is correct and that I have God's support and encouragement to state this publicly and emphatically. (See *'What are the Revelations and Inspired Messages from God?* Appendix 1, and *'Are the Revelations…the Truth from God?'*) Let us consider where the Tears from God historically come from when considering the three example religions of Christianity, Islam, and Hinduism.

Christianity has long believed in this phenomenon with it often being referred to as the 'gift of tears' from the Holy Spirit (God). The Holy Spirit freely gives charismatic gifts. Ewing beautifully encapsulates the closeness with God caused by these Tears when she highlights how the Holy Spirit is infused into the receiver's soul. The action of the Tears is the physical sign and personal experience of this bringing about such a result. The person will often be unable to explain what is or has happened - that the experience is somewhat subconscious and in a different realm.

Fenelon states how Pope Francis refers to these as 'the gift of tears'. He emphasises how this helps prepare the receiver to see Jesus (God), and how the concept is based on the 'Spiritual Exercises' of St Ignatius, especially where Ignatius is overwhelmed by the consolation of God. *The Tears are coming from a sense of deep intimacy with God, primarily while Ignatius celebrated the Eucharist in all its beauty and the presence of God's love.* He goes on to share theologian Tim Muldoon's thoughts on how the pope sees this as *a mystical experience of a deep, preconscious conviction of God's presence. It results from an overwhelming experience of receiving God's intimate love, which can only be expressed through free-flowing tears.*

*Before **Heaven**: Hints Tips Stories*
Bryan Foster

Fr Bartunek, who was an evangelical Christian and is now a Catholic priest, explains that this gift can occur singularly or on multiple occasions. He states that it doesn't mean the receiver is any holier or any closer to God than others. *He says it is an event to encourage those receiving or witnessing it to be in more significant and more substantial relationships with God.* It provides excellent comfort from God or confirms decisions that they had previously made, as well as a defense against temptation. Physiologically, Bartunek notes how these Tears from God are not like every day healthy tears resulting when someone is sobbing due to normal life's emotions. These tears flow abundantly and freely without any physical tension or facial contortions. *He also mentions that this gift isn't in scripture or the Catechism but has been referred to by various spiritual writers ever since the beginning of the early church.*

In Al-Islam, examples of *Tears from God are seen in both the Qur'an and traditions.* Some examples in the Qur'an include *when tears occur as a sign of perceiving the realities of God or as a sign of wisdom. Prophets shed tears for Allah when hearing of communications from God.* Tears are seen as so significant in Islamic tradition that *they are a gift to humanity, illuminate and soften the heart and bring about a great reward from God, including extinguishing God's wrath.* Rattner speaks of what he calls the emotion of devotion, a crying for God, which he explores from both the Hindu and Christian traditions. Like both the Christian and Islamic examples above, *the Tears come from God at those special and often unique transformational moments with God.* These were regular and spontaneous, purifying him to experience higher states of consciousness, leading to his continual spiritual development. See the 'Tears from God' and sections A and B. Edited Extract from *Where's God? Revelations Today*, by Bryan.

*Before **Heaven**: Hints Tips Stories*
Bryan Foster

God-Given <u>UNIQUE</u> Sun Signs, Sun Arrows, Sun Flares, and a Giant Easter Sun Cross, Attracts Us – Stunningly.

*** <u>Look for sun arrows, sun flares, and twinkling sun.</u> ***

<u>Images Challenge</u>: Look for sun arrows going to and over me in both images, one above, and two on the next two pages. These sometimes need real concentration, but each arrow and flare are there in the Images!!! Observe the flares shooting off the sun and 'firing' the arrows. See also the beautiful sparkling sun rays. These two images are very Unique, don't you think?

Before **Heaven**: Hints Tips Stories
Bryan Foster

Book 4, a photobook, introduces genuine, UNIQUE God-given images not seen before by most people. I hadn't seen anything similar myself. *These are raw, spectacular, unique, and untouched images.* The images were taken on an android phone. It is highly recommended to have Book 4 handy when reading Books 3 and 5. Or at least having read/viewed Book 4 prior to the other *Series'* books.

Book 4 is my favourite, as it shows so much more about God and God's methods of attracting people to 'His' divine, holy, powerful, and loving Words – through photography. *God's use of photographic images is something extra special and necessary to engage people in what God is offering – Absolute Love and Forgiveness worldwide.*

The Signs/Images are Unique & Brilliant!!! WOW!!! Genuine, Real, and New. Also, Startling Images! (Book 4)

Book 2 has the first sun image used in this *Series* as its cover pic. It is a relatively smallish cloud appearing just above the peak of Mt Warning/Wollumbin, northern NSW. With close observation, you can see sun rays shooting out sideways and above the cloud.

*Before **Heaven**: Hints Tips Stories*
Bryan Foster

*Before **Heaven**: Hints Tips Stories*
Bryan Foster

The image above is presented in this Book 9 for more clarity of the image, without any text written over it, as does appear on the completed cover of this Book. It is the image on the cover image of Book 9, spread across front and back covers.

Book 4 has a brilliant **UNIQUE** image as its cover pic. (See next page)

This is of a giant Easter sun cross in the sky in 2018, just outside Texas on the **Qld/NSW** border in the north region of New South Wales.

It is a series of six images increasing the content on each image and taken quite quickly apart.

The final image resulted in a giant spectacular sun cross.

It began as the sun, then as a cross starting from the sun, then grow downwards, as the complete sun cross.

*Before **Heaven**: Hints Tips Stories*
Bryan Foster

Incidentally, the Cross was not seen on the mobile's (cellphone) camera until it was uploaded onto the laptop that evening. All I saw while taking the images was the sun and the cattle loading ramp.

See more of these images, including various photographic series in the order taken, on Facebook, in the 'God Today' group. What floored my wife and I, were the straight arrows coming from the flares attached to the sun.

I firmly believe that these were sent by God to help us all be challenged by some very stunning images based on and from the sun. And that these images are Unique and directly from God for our benefit! To then Trust fully in God and God's Divinity, Love and Forgiveness. God Truly LOVES us all Equally.

Book 4, also in particular, shows different types of spectacular sun arrows, (possibly never seen before by other people and me), where the sun arrows are being 'fired' from a sun flare protruding from the sparkling sun, coming through the rainforest canopy.

The reader needs to very carefully analyse the image to see the actual sun arrow getting closer to the author in each following image. These sun arrows appear to be moving to and through me.

However, and *to most people's amazement,* after checking the electronic date and times of each image, **the opposite occurs with the sun arrows. *These are receding away from me and appearing to return to the sun backward, with the arrowhead still facing me and the base of the arrow returning to the sun!!!***

The sun in these images is shining through the rainforest at various venues at and around Mt Warning/Wollumbin, NSW, Australia. I initially was only considering taking some selfies of the sun and me in the rainforest. However, *God did wonderful displays, which were once again only seen when these were uploaded onto the PC laptop.*

These sun arrows are from several different sites around the Scenic Rim of the old volcanic Mt Warning/Wollumbin, plus Southport, along with Vernon, BC, in Canada. The giant Easter sun cross (at Texas on the border of NSW and Qld); the sun cloud on Mt Warning/Wollumbin; and a double rainbow shining behind and 'across' my caravan while at Straddie; are examples of several other special and most unique images based on formations from the sun.

God-Given Unique Sun Signs Attract Us – Stunning, Genuine, Untouched Images

What do you do when you're taking selfies of yourself with the sun behind you, thinking that the sparkling sun as seen through the rainforest canopy was extra special in itself? To then not see any scenery difference on your mobile phone's screen. To have to wait, unbeknown to yourself, that all you needed to do was upload the images to your laptop back at camp! **So many images were UNIQUE.**

Once this has been done, it becomes one of those incredible moments in your relationship with God. You witness on the laptop's screen various extra special, original, and what appears as something spectacular and incredible from God for you. And it truly is real and for you from God.

As a result of this extra special moment in your relationship with God, over a few seconds, while taking six photographs on your mobile phone, just south of Texas in NSW, Australia, you capture the development of a large Easter sun cross one week after Easter Sunday on the next Sunday in 2018.

The giant cross is built from the sun, reaching across the sky and down to the earth as a gigantic cross. This was so magnificent and true that it is the cover image for the photobook, Book 4 in the '*God Today*' Series. All images in Book 4 are the exact images received on the camera. No Photoshopping or anything else, (except once – the Book 2 photobook cover pic with the cloud atop Mt Warning/Wollumbin – see previous comments.) Various images within Book 4 show the actual cross growing, from the normal sun shining in the sky, up to the completed Easter cross. (Most people seem to be referring to Book 4, the blue photobook, as 'the blue book', when drawing people's attention to this cross, along with other original sun creations from God.) The front cover is blue with a white cross and white book titles. The extra images of the cross developing from just the sun to the magnificent sun cross can be seen on pages 12-14 in Book 4.

(*Where's God? Revelations Today Photobook Companion: GOD Signs* (2nd *ed.*) by Bryan Foster, 2018.)

The next powerful set of images, also highlighted in Book 4 within the '*GOD Today' Series*, is equal to the giant sun cross or better?

These images show various sun flares, sun arrows, and sparkling sun, shining amongst the developing sun arrows shining through various foliage in the Mt Warning/Wollumbin rainforest in northern NSW, Australia. A couple of samples are shown just prior to this page. Once again seven images show a transition of the sun's effects on arrows, this time.

These unique images show the arrows appearing to be 'formed by the sun' travelling from the flare shooting out from the sun, through the atmosphere, and towards the author, also the selfie photographer. That is, you see seven images of the arrows from the sun's flares, travelling to contact me. **These are so unique, genuine, authentic, and extremely powerful. (See Book 4, pages: 7, 9, 18-19, 21, 28-29.)**

The purpose of receiving these sun images took quite an amount of time discerning each image and what the purpose of God was. Book 4 also includes other images which fit strongly into this category. *Incredibly, nobody else seems to have received these sun images from God that I am aware of so far.* (If any reader knows otherwise, I would very much like to contact these people.)

These images are so strong that it is hoped that most people will be challenged to grow exponentially toward God's presence through these images within their lives and within their enjoyment of this book's *Series*. Sometimes deep concentration is needed to see the sun arrows and other sun formations – but these are very much present, true, and definitely worth the challenge to see each one as presented by God for us.

Several people have reacted incredibly strongly to both seeing the arrows and not seeing these at first glance. For some, the need to search for the sun arrows and flares may take a little more time initially than expected, but there is nothing wrong with this type of search. It is my discerned belief that God wants us to explore as needed until these images are discovered and clearly seen by the reader. **Sometimes the more effort we give**

during this search, the greater the benefit will be, once the discoveries from God are found. These discoveries are not just from this Book 9 but are from all the books in this 10-book *Series*.

When this moment of discovery by the reader is achieved, it is my discerned belief that God wants us to use these findings to support 'His' Oneness with us all. His absolute perfect love for us individually. Remember, that it is the person who moves away from God that is the sinner. God never moves away from us. See that such spectacular images just described are real. Be open to what God offers us in this 10-book *'God Today' Series*.

Sun Images – Different Effects – Sun Arrows, Sun Cross, Double Rainbows

Also, recently, and three days after the experience above, I left my house, went outside, and for no reason at all, looked towards the sun, which was glowing from behind and through some shade cloth onto both Karen and me. The colours and clarity of my surroundings seemed quite different from the norm and were fully visible. Each object seemed to have a shimmering outline on its outside.

The colours blended differently from what is normally expected and seen. The colours were sharper in some places and lighter and almost thinning out in other positions. The colours looked more like an art piece, just off perfection but still outstandingly attractive and inspiring. Karen was with me, and she described the scene's appearance as normal for her. This clarified that we were both viewing the same image, but that it was being seen differently by each of us. As many 3D images normally are in the real world.

This highlights that God inspires and advises us on our direction and activities for 'Him'. These will likely be the same or different for us all. Sometimes Karen sees exactly as I do; on other occasions, her viewing images are slightly different. What is your experience yourself?

The more we see and interpret what is becoming visible around us, the more we realise that there are many very special moments and incidents God is working us towards. *The more we can truthfully say, "Yes!", to God, the closer we are becoming to God, and the sooner we will hopefully experience God as The One.* God is the One and Only God existing in any genuine religion, anywhere, anytime, at any place in history. Once again, be open to the Only God of the universe. Throughout all time!

Book 4 (Photobook). Many UNIQUE Photographic Images from God. Assists Considerably with Bryan's credibility.

The use of photographic signs is significantly highlighted in the photobook, Book 4, *Where's God? Revelations Today Photobook Companion: GOD's Love* (2018). It is in themed sets, with the sun being central, along with other associated nature images taken by the author. To view these sun creations from God, see the author's two main websites at:

https://www.godtodayseries.com

https://www.bryanfosterauthor.com

*Before **Heaven**: Hints Tips Stories*
Bryan Foster

Bryan, also has a number of these at <u>God Today | Facebook</u>

These specific sun arrow images started in the rainforest, which surrounds the carpark used by the climbers of Mt Warning/Wollumbin, northern NSW, Australia. These were initially taken as standard photographic images. After a few were taken, he soon changed into taking some selfie images of the sun and himself, as the sun sparkled brightly through the early morning rainforest canopy. Initially to Bryan, he was not initially aware of the *sun arrows, and sun flares'* inclusions becoming a genuine part of the images eventually displayed in Book 4 - *Where's God? Revelations Today Photobook Companion: GOD's Love* (2018). The sun and additions were not revealed to both of us until the images were uploaded to our laptop at day's end! As the photos were taken, the sun arrow and sun flare images from God were not apparent. Then these were real and very apparent and caused us to be totally 'gob-struck' once opened on our laptop.

Due to the MAGNITUDE and UNIQUENESS of the SUN and SUN ARROWS' inclusions, Book 4 (photobook) becomes an essential read for anyone interested in God, God's ways, God's Revelations and Inspired Messages, unforgettable images of the sun, sun arrows, sunrays, sun flares, a giant sun cross taken outside Texas in New South Wales, on the border of NSW and southern Queensland, double rainbows, etc. (See some of the Unique Images in this Book 9.)

Over the next couple of years, this type of collection of images, including God's special inclusions, was continued. Each collection encouraged us so much to share God's creativity to help us find God, believe in God, and use God's creativity to help make people universally become aware of God's authentic reality and the massive assistance God can be for genuine believers.

This unique approach using the photographic images sent from God to us, helps to encourage the reader to search for God's intimacy in their own lives. We can then start seeing more of God and God's actions in our everyday world. *This is us becoming one with God on Earth and leads to a higher level of 'Heaven' on Earth, guiding us to how we approach our lives to be pure of heart and mind at our death.* Heaven, God, and us together after death, is still an unknown existence for our discovery, but...?

UNIQUE Images Draw Us Closer to God

I believe that this is God encouraging us to go that much further with His Revelations, etc. It is something like – you LOVE these UNIQUE and CHALLENGING photos, now **love all the Revelations and Inspired Messages from God – because these are very special and directly from God to us!!!** *Love is at the forefront of everything we do. Heaven awaits us all, if we continue our spiritual development prior to and immediately after our deaths in preparation to be with God for eternity.*

Book 4 is highlighted due to its High Significance in Assisting God to Proclaim various Revelations and Inspired Messages for Today, photographically. The images are literally often beyond this world and directly from God. Each image is authentically real. Many are genuinely UNIQUE. (See samples in this Book 10 on p. 99 and 101.) (Only one image needed colour enhancement, due to the light rays being somewhat too light to be obviously seen when printed. It is the cover of Book 2.)

Viewing Book 4's images, while reading throughout the Series, adds so much to the reader's appreciation and love of the Divine God. So many unique and special images from God, to encourage us to believe in God's Revelations and discerned Inspired Messages, given to us in this ten-book series, 'God Today' Series.

Book 4 – Author's Favourite.

The UNIQUE, CHALLENGING, and INCREDIBLY SPECTACULAR images, are my favourite visual inputs from God within this Series. God truly is one with those who see these arrows.

The more I see these images, the greater importance for us all, I feel these to be. **It is not just the UNIQUENESS and GIFTS from God of the images that count. It is a form of proof of God's presence and support for this Series.** *I had considerable divine input and support from God while composing this book Series.* All the examples just mentioned, and more, are on full display in Book 4,

(*Where's God? Revelations Today Photobook Companion: God's Signs,* (2018), Bryan Foster, Great Developments Publishers, Gold Coast.)

In the images, count the arrows and flares especially.

For the Easter Cross (see p.67), it took six images to show the gigantic sun cross developed to this final image.

Before **Heaven**: Hints Tips Stories
Bryan Foster

All *'God Today' Series* books are available from internet bookstores and some shopfront bookshops.

To continue with the surprises and uniqueness of these images, could you possibly believe that the seven images of the sun arrows appearing to go from the sun's flare to Bryan, are actually going backwards towards the sun, and not the normally expected, forward maneuver. This was only found when checking the written details of each image attached to each electronic photo.

Challenges at Death and Just After Death

'Heaven' on Earth with God's Love

Why wait for death and arrival in Heaven? We can experience examples of 'Heaven on Earth' when we are remarkably close to God, primarily through prayer and a genuine loving lifestyle with God leading along to positive, loving relationships. We have the divine encouragement of God to do what is Right and Good, to start our development toward Heaven here while still on Earth!

This then continually develops towards our death moment, where we have the choice, along with God, at death to continue our existence, whether in Heaven or Hell. (The possibility of Purgatory for Catholics is still quite probable. And hence for other variations, if any, as well.)

This ninth book in the *'GOD Today' Series* – continues the journey of discovering God's Love that began with *1God.world: One God for All* and *Where's God? Revelations Today*, along with

*Before **Heaven**: Hints Tips Stories*
Bryan Foster

each of these two Book's photobook companions. I renew and continue further the exploration of who God is, what essentials Love, and Forgiveness are, and how God can be discovered and followed. I build on the twenty-six personal stories of the spiritual discovery of God in Book 1 and the twelve Revelations from God in Book 3.

Interestingly, because of the AUTHENTIC and literally GENUINE UNIQUENESS and the challenge of many images in Book 4, these God's creative images hopefully inspire us to be challenged to believe the Truth of the Revelations that do very much come directly from God. *It is God doing what God does – no force or cohesion exerted.*

Through viewing the fascinating, UNIQUE photographic images created by God, we encourage ourselves and others to be directed towards God, personally and communally.

Before **Heaven**: *Hints Tips Stories*
Bryan Foster

Be very ready!!!

There are also a minimal number of people who don't know God for whatever reason. These people cannot, therefore, reject God as they don't know God or about God. We should imagine that if these people lead good lives, then most likely they will go to Heaven. Especially as they can't sin without knowing God and God's ethics for us. Timing? Unknown. But they should eventually get there. They can certainly do wrong and can have these forgiven out of love.

Each existence is through our relationship with God, along with our own personal choice now at death, which depends so much on how we lived and where we place our existence with God.

The largest Christian religion, Catholicism, also believes in another alternative existence after death. It is called Purgatory. Followers of this belief believe that only those who are perfect will enter Heaven. They believe that if at death the person isn't pure or seriously evil, and is knowing of and believing in God, then they will go to an existence known as Purgatory until they become pure in Love. This makes considerable sense going on the definitions of God and Heaven and who will end up living a perfect existence forever. But what has become commonly known and probably believed by most Catholics, is that only those close to God, close to perfection, get straight into Heaven with God. You would sense that a large cohort of Catholics, and possibly many other non-Catholics, influenced by this belief, will progress through Purgatory at their deaths.

At death, have we ended up being very loving, very hate-filled, or a mixture of good and bad? If during a person's life one feels all the bad things in life are the best for them, then they will more than likely lean to the evil side and then be affected to such a degree that they will choose evil and the rejection of God, at death, because that is the lifestyle which they enjoyed the most, while alive on earth. They most likely will now, after death, reject God, whether God was known or not. And choose evil because that suits them now, as it did through much of their lives. Through our lives of Love or hate will come our decision. Love God or Freely Reject the known and Absolutely Loving God.

Out of Absolute Love and Free Will for humanity,

God shares the final choice in our after-death destination. God has been with each of us full-time throughout our lives. Not leaving each of us for even a second. Offering guidance to Us all, and subsequently to Salvation with God in Heaven.

Our lifestyles are critical for Salvation with God or otherwise. God is there at that time when each person offers their favoured decision. Now that is Love for Everyone. Each makes their personal decision based on their former pre-death lifestyle and their Love or Rejection of their known and understood God. Their behaviour and belief point Towards Their After Death Choices to be close or away from God! It is believed that God considers their views and then makes the final choice of people's final destination.

*Before **Heaven**: Hints Tips Stories*
Bryan Foster

Lovers Mostly LOVE GOD!

Haters Mostly Hate or REJECT GOD!

GOD LOVES THE LOVERS AND HATERS - Equally!

Haters freely turn away from God.

Lovers freely turn towards God.

GOD ONLY LOVES.

GOD LOVES EACH HUMAN, Fauna and Flora Creations

EACH CHOOSES Heaven or Hell!

GOD INVITES ALL OF CREATION TO HEAVEN!

ALL OF THE CREATION CHOOSES HEAVEN OR HELL!

*Before **Heaven**: Hints Tips Stories*
Bryan Foster

Humans, Plants and Animals (+ probably all created inert/non-life objects) – can go to Heaven.

Humans, Plants, and Animals will have the opportunities to get back to God in Heaven at death. As will all life creations from God. This would be considered relatively, or fully, new by most people and religions. Plus, all created inert objects from God, may also possibly get to Heaven, after all living creations have died (or before…, depending on God's decisions). Those receiving these sacred messages required me, and no doubt others, to pass these on to the religious leaders, religious scholars, and holy people of today's religions, who will be able to discover how and why this occurs, through their closeness with God and other religious leaders, scholars, theologians, scripture experts, etc. As they would do for any other Revelation or inspired message from God.

For me, this belief is a discerned Inspired Message from God. It is true. Why? Because God said it was over many years for me. Tears from God often occurred also, etc., and this no doubt happened to others alike, worldwide. This shows how something will religiously inspire and possibly challenge us in a necessary divine encounter often quite regularly. Too many times, too many people ignore, deny, or even miss the experience that God had just given them. **Be open to exploring what might be, or is, God's presence in your lives. Be prepared for something different when God comes to you spiritually. These times become your very special God times!**

Before **Heaven**: *Hints Tips Stories*
Bryan Foster

Remember that old joke/message, where a floundering, sinking sailor deep out to sea, wanted to be rescued? He was a true lover of God! He kept calling to God to save him. God sent a submarine, which he refused. God then sent a giant tanker, which was also refused. Finally, God sent a helicopter, which was once again refused. When God asked the sailor why he didn't take one of the ships or the helicopter sent, he said he prayed to God to save him and was just waiting for God to rescue him. He totally missed God's three rescue attempts. **We need to be open so as not to miss or reject God's approach to us.** *We must always be open to receiving God in whatever way God wishes to communicate with us. Listen, reflect, pray, meditate to find God…*

Many people find that being open to anything divine, supernatural, or spiritual, becomes an invitation to God to come to them. I certainly agree, primarily due to both my wife's and my personal experiences, when God makes Himself known to us e.g., often through the Tears of God sent to us that we both received. As people's experiences grow more frequently with God over time, they will learn much about God and God's living creations, both fauna and flora. They will start to become much more Godlike, e.g., being open to God's Love and God's Truth, through prayer, meditation, forgiveness, compassion, empathy, justice, growth, spirituality, lifestyles, and Godliness, etc., and living and exemplifying God's Love for all of creation.

These are characteristics/descriptors of God and from God for each of us! It is how we are 'made in the image of God'. *These images of God, in which we are made, are not physical ones but ones that use those special Godly loving characteristics: e.g., feelings, emotions, forgiveness, compassion, directions, strength and power for good, etc. from God.*

Before **Heaven**: *Hints Tips Stories*
Bryan Foster

Some of these Absolute qualities of God are Love, Forgiveness, Compassion, and Wisdom, etc. This belief gets quite confused at times. We must remember that there are no physical looks from our human perspective. Divinity is far beyond the physical. God is Divine, we are physical!

The one exceptional reality I am incredibly humbled by and freely and honourably accept from God has been the real, genuine Revelations, and Inspired Messages received and discerned. These have become very frequent while authoring these books, now in the eighth year *(Revelations were given by God to the author in 1982, 2016, 2018, and 2022/3).*

The questions most asked are, how do I get the Revelations from God? Does God talk to me? There are a few ways that this happens. However, for me, the 1st Revelations in 1982 (came at during a secondary school's 'Commitment to God' Day). The next two groups of Revelations in 2016 (15 Revelations from God), and in 2018 (6 Revelations from God), were received during the night, in the early morning hours around 3am on both occasions. This means I was awakened. Both times I was camping in a caravan/trailer at two different venues on the plains, of Mt Warning, NSW, Australia.

Once awoken, I received the messages from God in my 'mind's eye'. How? It is sort of like becoming part of my thoughts - yet not being my thoughts. If awake and adequately aware, you know the difference too. *In 2016 I was even told to, "Don't overthink what's happening, just write it down," after I paused a few times trying to get all this together.* And so, I did. These were the 15 Revelations from May 2016. I usually get the 'Tears from God' as one form of proof, yet not for this occurrence in 2016. This time it wasn't until the next day at a First Communion Mass in the local church where Karen and I were married that it occurred.

I asked God if the last night's 15 Revelations were real, and the answer was obviously, "Yes!" I received these very tearfully -

'Tears from God' during the Eucharistic celebration as God's main proof of authenticity of the Revelations.

The 2018 Revelations were on a different camping ground but relatively close by, this time at the foot of Mt Warning/Wollumbin (the first people's name for this mountain).

Yet, God told me these, and I received each Revelation in the same way as I did 2.5 previous years ago for the first 15 Revelations.

These six are numbered #16 to #21. Hence, I had now received 21 Revelations from God in 2016 and 2018, plus the original as a teacher at a secondary school in Brisbane Australia in 1982. These are referred to as the 21+1.

Or 21 +1 (or +2 when including the 2022 Revelation from God - if it was a Revelation.)

*Before **Heaven**: Hints Tips Stories*
Bryan Foster

Author's Medical Issues – A Possible Starting Point You May Like to Use for Growing Closer to God in a community? Life's Health Challenges and Healings, Help Us Find God and Love God!

We all have medical issues of various kinds, at various levels and at different ages, along with different medical and other support structures. Let us now progress further with the evaluation of some illnesses and injuries and how a person's illnesses and injuries may be some of yours, or similar to these, as well. These are the issues discussed here, but why? Mainly because as a starting point, these are the ones I know a fair bit about, because these are some of my medical experiences, and maybe like some of your ones, as well. *This section was written to hopefully assist any reader interested in how we deal with their serious or chronic illnesses and injuries. And where these lead us during the illnesses and after the illnesses. All this leads us to become one with God throughout our lives. Trusting in God to care for us deeply, which God does! Also remembering that God may make different decisions than what we would like.*

Firstly, to be aware of the obvious that most people have various chronic illnesses and injuries. Some are serious, others not. These might often be chronic but not deadly. Or acute and deadly? Etc.

I have been so pleased over my lifetime to have many people who were prepared to assist and guide my family and me through various illnesses and injuries. Having such people is absolutely essential once you know how helpful their assistance is for us. Having people to talk about various issues, illnesses, and injuries, is so comforting and healing at times, along with being helpful for encouraging the seeking of professional medical advice when needed. It is out of Love, that God encourages us to keep going, not give up, and look for solutions from the medical fraternity, other people, and our own personal experiences. As well as continually asking God for help through these medical issues.

Some processes actioned for various illnesses I have or had, may hopefully give you some help to assist in your possibly similar progress to improve your health issues; if this is what you'd like to help support you. You may be able to assist me health-wise through comments on my websites or Facebook's 'God Today' page. If you were anything like me, as you progress through the highs and lows of life, you seek advice, along with hints and tips on health from an often-large source of people, medical or otherwise. Many of our reactions and responses have come from suggestions from family, friends, and colleagues. A key point often rejected or just dismissed by some people, unfortunately, this includes mostly males, is that they often ignore the need for professional medical advice early on with the illness or injury. Many do not even seek it, when everything cries out for them to do so! Often, this is not until the last or later moment, before things can go haywire, if there is still time?

We all have our unhealthy/illness list. It is what we do with it that counts. The following are offered as just one person's example with several mild to serious illnesses needing healing over several years, so that life can stay enjoyable and goes on at the best health level available under our individual circumstances. **Continually ask God for help.** *God strongly supports highly qualified medical people due to their high levels of training and knowledge built up over generations for us all. We need to genuinely thank God for His chosen solution for each of us and worked through our doctors and other medical assistants.*

*Before **Heaven**: Hints Tips Stories*
Bryan Foster

I believe it is important to know that even with a number of these illnesses/injuries over the years, I was in fact still quite fit and healthy and **at times, unaware of my true unhealthy condition. These conditions don't just impact unhealthy people.** Like many others, I also discovered that you successfully work and live with many of the health issues that you have.

A Suggested Major Hint: *If possible, surround yourself with experts in medicine, and work in consultation with your chosen medical team as the need determines. A good GP is essential as the coordinator with your other health professionals.* **Friends, work colleagues, neighbours, etc., could all play a positive part in your health and well-being.** *One such neighbour literally saved my life, by encouraging me to get to the hospital ASAP.* **He was correct. I was having a heart attack.** *Everything flowed together and I met the specialist doctor who was to be my cardiologist there. He has been my specialist for the 8 years since the event.*

I have always followed my father's advice about insurance, particularly health insurance – get it! (If at all possible!!!) Insurances are for all lifestyles and life things, e.g., cars, houses, content, life, health, careers, etc. I strongly believe that, if possible, it's best to have it. **Insurance allows so many possibilities from private to public medical care.** These insurances have saved many people, including myself, thousands of dollars throughout our lives. Yet, if you, the reader has differing views, and you feel comfortable with these differences, then that decision is obviously yours. We all must totally respect our hopefully informed decision, after our appropriate medical consultations, even if we are challenged by it. *Seeking medical advice is not a sign of weakness, it is a sign of strength. God gave us science and technology to help us through our lives.* These are outstanding gifts to each of us equally.

Before **Heaven**: *Hints Tips Stories*
Bryan Foster

Medical and health professionals become more important for each of us as we grow older. Not forgetting that it is also very important when we are younger and being threatened by serious health issues.

There were key medical experts who treated me before and after my 42 years of teaching before retirement. After retirement, *I became a full-time author of non-fiction texts, photobooks, websites and videos, having been a part-time writer and relief teacher for my last three years of teaching. My books cover four main themes: God; a Beginner's Guide to Caravanning; places to stay and things to see and do, while caravanning throughout Australia; plus, Photobooks highlighting spectacular places throughout Australia.* These are shared to help the reader become aware, if they are not already, of their possible need for medical treatment when similar or other medical challenges confront them. No matter how insignificant you may think it is, from my experience, it is often the best option to gain a medical opinion initially from your GP or from hospital doctors. Building a good relationship with your GP is probably the most significant response to illnesses or injuries and for keeping you healthy and fit. Especially as you start to age around retirement.

I personally shared stories here, and in my everyday life, with interested people, and they with me, to somewhat help with our decisions, however possible. *Over the years, I very much appreciated the assistance from others, especially family, friends, and colleagues, who suggested I have 'something' that needed to be investigated, etc.*

Mental Health. Mmmm, the topic we all seem to keep very quiet. I was treated by a psychiatrist and psychologist for quite some time with each, with a concentration occurring before my retirement, while I was still full-time teaching. I can honestly say how these two experts very much helped me with some extremely difficult choices, of which now I am so appreciative to have made and have my proper life back again after so many years. The psychiatrist advised that my condition was mainly formed through not getting over various health issues of varying levels, that I had for about a decade.

Unfortunately, the healing process included retiring from my very much-loved vocation of teaching in Catholic secondary (34 years) and primary schools (8 years) over 42 years and being a school and parish leader in a variety of ways.

I had a heart attack a few years back, and still have various chronic illnesses and injuries. These are my toughest remaining major illnesses. I can state without any doubt that if you have serious chest pains, ring 000 or 911 (or whatever the emergency number is in your country) or get straight to a hospital if you are close. Ambulances in most circumstances are the best solution, if possible. Check known present symptoms with your doctor or cardiologist for their suggestions if you are on the track for a heart attack!

An angioplasty operation in the heart (repairing a major blocked heart artery using a stent) occurred also in the past few years. I have been advised that other artery blockages will probably need serious repairs down the years. I am not keen on a possible major heart operation any time now. Best to be prepared though. *We all need to keep on top of various health issues for our health and fitness.* Our GP/hospital is usually the first point of contact to go to for an initial appraisal and treatment. When needed, you will have to see a specialist doctor, whom the GP or hospital emergency doctor will refer you to from his/her recommended specialist/s list e.g., an essential specialist for our heart is a cardiologist. *I also try not to leave everything to the doctor.* ***It is my life, my body, my illness or injury, and my decision on how it should all be treated medically, within reason. The final decision is yours, the patient. But the expert is the doctor.*** **Make well-balanced decisions, based on the best medical science available to you.** In most worldly cases, we probably make some of the final decisions, yet with *the doctor's highly qualified option/s, are our main choice of advice. Ignore their advice at your peril.*

Melanoma cancer can be deadly. It was surgically removed last year. These seem to be becoming more prevalent for me. In Australia especially, we need regular skin checks by doctors specialising in the skin, GP experts, or dermatologist specialists. My latest one was on my face and apparently quite large and serious. Plus, other skin cancers on the face and elsewhere over my body. Doctors started treating these skin cancers with frozen nitrogen spray, various medications in a tube from the chemist, or small cut-outs in surgery when I was 17 years of age. Various forms of skin cancer removals have continued up until the present day, including melanoma. **These sorts of medical treatments still happen to me today, after so many years – from age seventeen to mid-sixties.** Obviously, we all need to respect the sun and keep covered as best as we can, especially with creams, clothing, and other sun protection.

Now is the time for me to pay the price of Australian summers, where little regard was given to sun and skin protection when we were young. No doubt also in other countries where people do or did spend large amounts of time in the sun, without any, or with little protection. Up to decades after these sun cancer issues and prognoses became very common for me, we were

*Before **Heaven**: Hints Tips Stories*
Bryan Foster

treated well, fortunately. In our younger days, our knowledge and that of our parents about skin cancer and its impact on us was relatively unknown, or not seen in the same light as today.

Suffering a serious lower back injury at a mining factory when in my late teens, virtually commenced my lifelong back issues. I also had my blood poisoned, possibly picked up when I slipped and fell on wet ground outside a toilet block in a caravan park. I stayed in the hospital for 15 days until healed. Possible prostate issues arose not long ago. But now seems quite good as I don't have any symptoms now. *We're continually told that men should seriously have prostate check-ups and PSA blood tests regularly. It is often stated to be the Australian males' most common cause of death.*

Other surgeries have also occurred over the years, mostly on broken or damaged joints or ligaments, etc. Medications, diet, and physical training with GP and specialist doctors' guidance, and often physiotherapists too, help sustain and extend our lives, when treated by the right GPs and specialists and other allied health professionals at the right times. I visit a very special and highly trained physiotherapist regularly, due to my specific health needs, based on several previously mentioned medical and health issues in this article.

Obviously, we need to be aware of teeth care, particularly when playing contact sports. I lost two teeth in primary school playing football. Common sense says that mouthguards are essential, for at least contact sports.

Having received head knocks, some harder than normal, playing rugby league football and/or basketball from 8 to 20 years of age, could lead to brain injuries. Brain damage from these sorts of sports is now becoming common research, as the medical and sporting fraternity finally discuss and research what is now in the open. In Australia and the USA, they have started to implement precautionary preparations beforehand, mid-game treatments, and post-game treatments, etc.

How many years do you think we have before the various types of football (and other sports where the player's head is impacted forcibly?) are shut down and banned – all for our health's sake? Boxing and Octagon fights are probably at the top of the list?

What will the warriors in their teens to their thirties, do then? Is there a compromise that assists with playing the game and defending the head!? Along with much detailed research on both dead and living players to find the best methods and treatments to continually improve outcomes within these contact sports. **Brain injuries are one of the last things we should ever receive. These injuries impact so much on our lives, especially the older we get.**

We need to be so careful how we prepare for these with good medical help. **Trust in the medical fraternity is a good initial point in which to start the treatment for the remainder of our lives.**

Don't leave God out of these situations. Go to God as often as you can. Learn what is best for you from God and from others God works through. Love God deeply!

Follow as much of the above to do with your health, as you feel best doing. Or you may like to use the suggestions as a guide. Hopefully, some of these stories and suggestions will help you, as you travel along this road of life to God in Heaven. **Share with us some of your health stories through Facebook's, 'God Today' page or our websites. We can all learn from each other.**

God gave humanity science and technology for these various important medical and health findings and solutions. *You may feel the natural need to pray to God for strength, wisdom, and assistance, depending on your circumstances.* **It is stating the obvious, I realise, yet it is very important to especially work with your medical people towards your healing outcomes.**

We often find God in the pain and suffering within our and others' lives. Hopefully, many readers who considered themselves and their circumstances while reading this section, were able to find likenesses with my health stories. This may lead to their own health stories being examined and contemplated, and various healings considered and shared with others. **Let's work together with other people who can help us, guide us and in their own ways, love us!**

Necessary Medical Treatment ASAP

Each of these health issues, and any number more over the years, have certainly helped me in my understanding of life, illness, self-care, medical advice, treatment, death, life after death, etc. If nothing else, *these illnesses have been shared to try and inspire others to do what is required for their best health, especially when they are reticent to seek medical help.* **When it comes to seeking medical advice, it is often needed as soon as possible, once ill or injured.**

Leaving medical attention too late is often the quickest way to go downhill and lose the advantage of knowing you have an illness or other health issues and finding out what you need to do for healing. Some would say that my quickness to receive medical treatment is going too far beyond the anticipated timeline and as done by many in today's world. **On the contrary, I believe, the timing is best to go quickly than to lose the race to full health due to a false appreciation of when to see a doctor.** Males, in general, seem to search out medical help much slower than females. Not good.

However, there seems to be a change worldwide over the past few years, for men to start realising the necessity to at least see a GP in the first instance, and specialists later, if needed.

I SUGGEST AND RECOMMEND

DON'T IGNORE MEDICAL ADVICE.

SEEK ADVICE WHEN NEEDED.

LISTEN TO OTHERS YOU TRUST

WHO MIGHT BE VALUABLE IN HELPING YOU SELECT THESE MEDICAL PEOPLE WELL?

FIND A GOOD GP DOCTOR

AND/OR HOSPITAL

FOR YOUR PARTICULAR HEALTH NEEDS.

YOUR GP WILL BE ABLE TO ASSIST & COORDINATE HERE.

DON'T DELAY.

Medical Disclaimer

As much as I would like to help those with an interest in the above prognoses and healing methods, etc.,

I am not a doctor or health professional.

I am a book writer.

Hopefully, I might spark some interest in some people through seeing similarities between both the reader's and my illnesses and health conditions. Optimistically, this would begin a medical response to heal you, as it mostly did for me.

The suggestions given were included to –

*strongly encourage the reader to seek professional medical help from **GPs** and specialist doctors, and other allied health professionals, as and when the need arises.*

And especially to not delay.

*Before **Heaven**: Hints Tips Stories*
Bryan Foster

God is the Primary Bibliographical Source for the '*God Today*' Series!!!

God's Absolute Love and Truth

The genuine and authentic Truth of God's historical Revelations, as well as those new ones revealed to me (and most probably) others worldwide for today, must prevail. **Any Revelations I receive from God, along with any Discerned Inspired Messages from God, by their very nature are the Truth, hence no regular bibliographic reference is required. God is the Primary Source throughout!**

As an example, using my own religion's leaders, various Church leaders' groups have been sent books from the *Series*: Pope Francis; a Gold Coast visiting missionary along with a senior Parish Priest; the Australian Catholic University; the Executive Director of the local Brisbane Catholic Education Office (now retired); the local archdiocesan bookstore; along with a large commercial secular bookstore in Brisbane.

Yet, in the appreciation of my religious academic study to master's degree level; teaching senior school years 11 and 12 the 'Study of Religion' board subject for 30 years; teaching over 42 years different combinations of classes, subjects, and grades through 1-12, this was a fantastic background introduction for me to this *'God Today' Series*. Along with writing books, blogs, and articles, plus the Revelations sent to me directly from God in 1982, 2016, and 2018, (a 2022-3 possibility has just arrived, more on this last), along with numerous Inspired Messages from God over the decades, my lifetime of reflecting, praying, meditating, studying, and discussing at many and varied levels, have impacted very positively on me. What could these stories do for you, the reader, as well?

I believe these influential people and circumstances have supported me ideally to accept God's Revelations, Inspired Messages, information, directions, teachings, etc. for today's world – and to then share these with as many people as possible, as instructed by God.

God's Truth to Us + Evidence

God is Absolute Love.

God is Absolute Compassionate Love.

God is Absolute Forgiveness.

God is Absolutely gentle and Absolutely compassionate Love.

Obviously, God is not evil. God is aware of everything throughout time, space, and energy – before, during, and after anything that occurs within or for eternity.

God offers us Absolute Love, not for free, and not with a charge either, but to be earned by each of us separately and communally. Love breeds Love! Absolute Love takes us to another dimension, of which we weren't aware.

This was to assist each of us to aim for Heaven and Salvation. This is *Before Heaven* for which the book is titled and themed.

God uses tough, genuine Love, when the need arises.

Most harmful things people experience have been set up and freely decided somehow by some of humanity. Sometimes people are even unaware of doing so. Most pain and hardship we experience have often been freely chosen by people affected through their Free Will, and freedom from God. God does allow these painful and evil things to happen because these were freely decided by people, through God's Absolute Love and the Free Will of all impacts people!!! *Absolute Love Gives Absolute Free Will to Everyone*. People must make their own tough calls, both for the good of people and possibly unintentionally or with intention, causing unexpected and unwanted harm.

Due to Absolute Love, God must allow us to use our Free Will, to assist us to make the correct decisions for all. Only informed Rejectors of God won't make it to Heaven.

Just as the incarnate Jesus showed His tough love out of His respect for the Absolute Love of God in Heaven, he threw out of the Temple, those selling and exchanging money, so too must we educate and support people going astray to come back to God, fully and without reservation.

Sometimes we need to be firm in our respectful approach to others, who may lose their way to God and Heaven. We do this out of our authentic love of God and each other, so that as many people as possible will celebrate going to Heaven at their deaths. Are we a part of this whole absolute loving process with God?

*Before **Heaven**: Hints Tips Stories*
Bryan Foster

God's Absolute Love for All Creation.

God Is Absolute Love.

Being our Creator, this Love freely allows each of us to make our own decisions out of God's Love.

God will not force anyone to Believe,

or do anything without the Person's decision through their Free Will and Informed Conscience.

God's Absolute Love is showered on all people to help us decide what is best for each and every one -

past, now, and forever forward,

out of Genuine Respect and

our Love of God in return.

God's Love is so great,

that He wants every creation, fauna, flora, and probably even inert objects of His, to Go to Heaven!

Only the Evil, Informed about God Rejectors, Miss Out. Forever!!!

*Before **Heaven**: Hints Tips Stories*
Bryan Foster

Jesus and Mahomad – Are Both God Incarnate

Revelation #15 (from the 2016, 15 Revelations given from God to the author, Bryan Foster) acknowledges that:

Mahomad and Jesus are both Incarnations of God i.e., both are fully God and fully human. However, at different eras and places in history. **The unique, original transcript below is an image taken of Revelation 15, from 2016.**

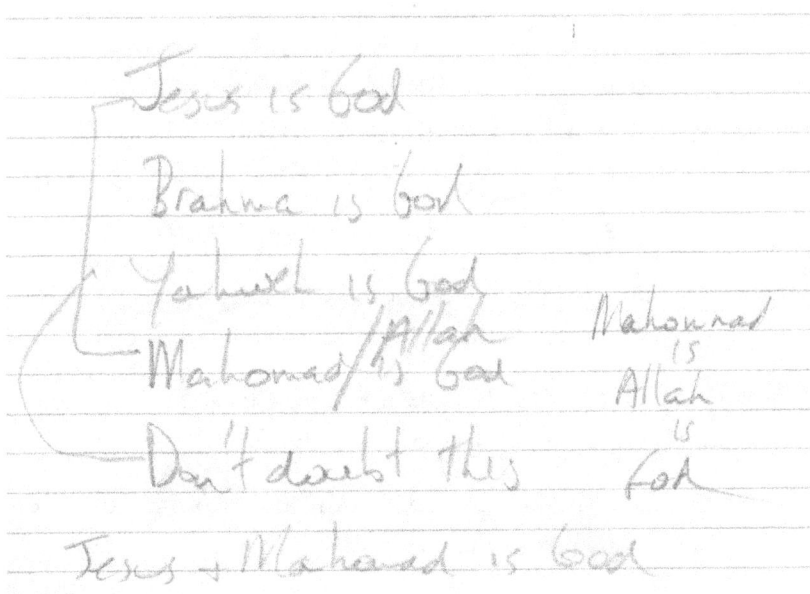

Muslims now should legitimately acknowledge that –

the prophet, *Mahomad, is also Allah/God.

Mahomad = Prophet = Allah = God.

Christians have always had Jesus, as a prophet who is God.

(* Mahomad spelled this way by God in the 2016's 15 Revelations, except for once.)

Revelations (R) from GOD to Bryan Foster for Today's World. Revelations in 1982 (1), 2016 (15) and 2018 (6). Plus, 100+ discerned Inspired Messages (IM) over Decades to the Author.

Referencing in this *Series'* books: Primary source = GOD. Secondary sources = books, articles, websites, and videos.

There is ONLY ONE GOD for all people, all religions, and all cultures-for all time - past, present, and future. (Rev. #10)

Jesus and *Mahomad are both Incarnations of GOD (* Spelling as mostly given by GOD to Bryan) (e.g. Rev. #15)

GOD IS ABSOLUTE LOVE (Revelation to Us all throughout history + Discerned by obviously many others worldwide.)

GOD says that we are ALL EQUAL and LOVED EQUALLY by GOD (Rev. #9, 2016).

Before *Heaven*: Hints Tips Stories
Bryan Foster

God's Revelations Book 3, Rev #1 to 12.

Book 5, Rev #6, #13, #14, #15, #16-21.

Book 9, Revelations #1 to #21 + 1 (or + 2, yet to be decided).

The bold type on the following three pages is added by the author as highlighting and is not part of God's 21 Revelations. It is used to specifically highlight NEW (R) or (IM) for all readers worldwide.

God's 21 Revelations to Us in 1982, 2016 and 2018. (Bold Type are the New Revelations for Us Today.)

The Revelations following are exact quotations from God. (Bold type from the author.)

1. **Be Truthful**
2. **Don't be Greedy**
3. Love life – don't take it
4. Respect all
5. Love one another as I have loved you
6. **Die for what is right.**
7. **Be educated for what is right & truthful**
8. Education is paramount for all
9. **We are One**
10. **One God Only One GOD**

"I am Prophet
Prophets are true"

Before **Heaven**: Hints Tips Stories
Bryan Foster

(This is close to the physical placement and punctuation in the transcribed Revelations received, i.e., after number ten and on the right lower side of the page. Is it referring to the author?

11. GOD's Messages to a world in need
12. This world is in enormous need
13. Cyberbullying - in all its forms of all sorts of all ages…
14. Fear rules – often from the cyber world eliminate this

15. **Jesus is God
Brahma/[n] is God
Yahweh is God
**Mahomad/Allah is God
**Don't doubt this
Jesus & Mahomad is God
Mahomad is Allah is God

Revelations #1-15 from 29 May, 2016, received on the plains at the foot of Mt Warning, Murwillumbah Showgrounds, NSW Australia, after being awoken at about 3am of the morning while staying in my caravan/trailer.

16. We NEED GOD
17. We need <u>to be vulnerable to God</u>
18. We need to continually be asking for GOD's help and assistance & support – always.
'No big heads' – just ask for help. Always.
19. We are insignificant compared to GOD.
20. GOD is so superior – face up to it
Believe it! Stop fighting it!
21. Be meek & humble & real

*Before **Heaven**: Hints Tips Stories*
Bryan Foster

Revelations #16-21 were received at Mt Warning Rainforest Park camping grounds at approx. 3am on 3 November, 2018.

GOD also sent me six Inspired Messages (IM) in the afternoon, before the 15 Revelations were received that upcoming night, on May 28, 2016.

1. GOD has permanent 'Tears from God'. Not from crying but from Absolute Love for all living creations. It is one form of proof for God's messages to the world.
2. GOD is not the warrior image.
[But the Absolute Love image.]
3. But is the loving, caring, for all others.
[Lover]
4. Our bodies are indeed the Temple of GOD.
[God is fully present with each of us.]
5. Purify [our bodies]
6. Don't harm, poison it[our bodies]…illicit drugs, smoking.

(Examples of these images may also be found on the GodTodaySeries.com and BryanFosterAuthor.com websites and the 'God Today' Facebook group page.)

Jesus and *Mahomad

Two Incarnations of God - Details

(Revelation #15 in 2016 to the Author)

This *Series'* last two books, Books 9 and 10, are a unique, truthful, narration of author articles, and God's Revelations and discerned Inspired Messages to the author, along with author stories necessary to bring the key questions and possible answers created and developed over seven-plus years, together in one place – for a significant Revelation from God for all humanity. It begins with an introduction, which includes essential themes to appreciate the claims made in this Book. Next comes the major claim about the TWO INCARNATIONS of GOD being explored. Following these challenging Revelations is a detailed breakdown of the last six Revelations given directly to the author by God but not yet detailed for the reader in any of this Series' publications.

As we are all at a variety of places in our relationship with God, Books 9 and 10 don't assume anything about each reader's experiences and journey to, and with, God. That is, apart from the significant personal explorations people may be making through reading copies of this Book's *Series* and other similar themed books available Today. Prayer is very important for the appreciation of God's Love and Messages for us all.

Revelation #15 is, I believe, the major Revelation for humanity, from the original series of Revelations revealed in May 2016, until now. It was not mentioned, being so as requested by God until the appropriate time. The timeline from God, which I was advised of during prayer, now places this book as the Ninth Book in the 'GOD Today' Series.

The time is now right to spread this most wonderful teaching from God.

This *Series* is the First Publication Worldwide of Revelation #15. **

(See Book 5 for Details - *Jesus and *Mahomad are God.*)

This is a magnificent addition to Islam and Christianity and our world. God has now told us that Jesus and Mahomad are both God/Allah, the One and the same God. Jesus and Mahomad are God Incarnate, i.e., both are fully God and fully human. (Revelation #15, 2016)

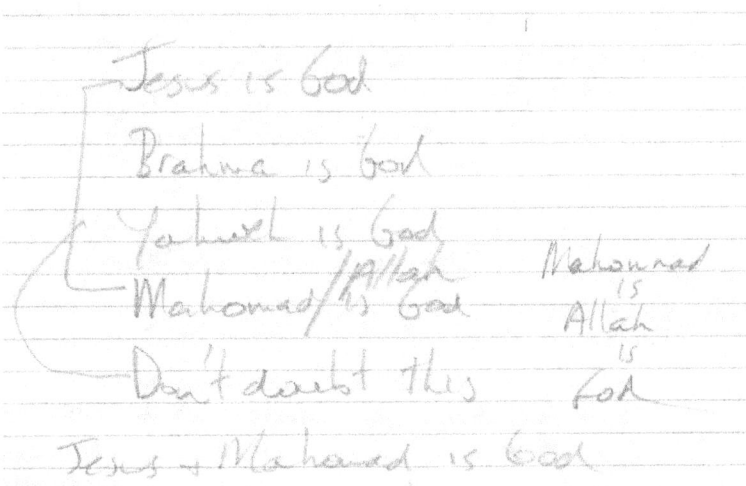

(*Mahomad spelled this way by God in the 21+1 Revelations, except for once.)

*Before **Heaven**: Hints Tips Stories*
Bryan Foster

Jesus and Mahomad need to assist us all worldwide, to help us all work together, and challenge each other as needed. People should never again use violence to support our supposed religious or spiritual differences. We are the same overall. We, Christians, and Muslims, have very similar divine information we both need, and hence we need to share this with each other. Both religions need to celebrate our prophets as if each was God/Allah, because they each are God=Allah, plus being fully human.

** (Of which I am aware).

Christians already do this i.e., with the Trinity, plus the key dogma of their religion, i.e., Jesus is fully God and fully human.

Now Islam needs to do the same. No longer is Mahomad to be seen only as a prophet. God/Allah has given humanity an absolutely, authentic, updated appreciation of who Mahomad is fully – Mahomad is both fully God and fully human. God has decided that such a magnificent additional belief for Islam is absolutely the Truth and essential for Islam today! God wants Muslims to believe this most incredible, divine growth of their religious beliefs of Mahomad. Through God's Revelations to the author in 1982, 2016, and 2018, we also see that modern-day prophets also legitimately exist. That these people selected also go through incredible positive and personal growth, doubt, and fear, as they have always done. That Mahomad wasn't the last prophet to exist.

This is a time for celebration as the One and Only God has told us that Jesus and Mahomad are equal. Islam and Christianity need to celebrate this. Don't cut it short but accept that this whole statement is absolutely the Truth from

God. Once we accept Revelation #15, that Jesus and Mahomad are God, and that this is definitely the Truth, then we can begin to work together to realign our beliefs, teachings, attitude to each other, attitudes to the One and Only God of eternity, etc.

Mahomad=Allah/God. Allah=God. We must Celebrate that Mahomad is Allah i.e., God. Only known as a prophet for centuries, God has now commanded that Mahomad is God. This has nothing to do with false prophets we are warned about historically! This is very real; very true and an essential major addition for all Muslims to celebrate and live with joy in their hearts and love within their soul and within their whole being!

Jesus=Mahomad. Mahomad=God. Jesus=God.

We are all asked to keep this in perspective.

(*Mahomad spelled this way by God in the 21+1 Revelations, except for once.)

Islam Must Celebrate Mahomad's Incarnation as God/Man/Prophet – said Allah/God

Without any Violence. Violence is Wrong and Must Be Stopped!

God Rejects Violence, except in self-defense, when minimal force is allowed to protect the harmed person or people.
Good Changes Can, and Must be Made -

*Before **Heaven**: Hints Tips Stories*
Bryan Foster

WITHOUT VIOLENCE!

Allah=God=Absolute Love=No Inappropriate or Illegal Violence.

We now need to be in search of each of our scriptures, teachings, beliefs, theologies, etc. to bring both our legitimate and Truthful religious institutions and God's teachings together as one.

There is absolutely no reason for violence or unfair dismissal of any of our differing, yet strongly similar, beliefs and teachings.

God=Allah.

God=Allah=Yahweh=Brahma/n (See scripture pages for detail in the Contents table.)

Readers are asked to respect this updated publication of Revelation from God. The release may possibly cause considerable discussion, acceptance, or denial, and possibly some readers will be overcome by emotion and even some possible grief to its Truth and place in our religious world.

Any belief which says that God can't change anything already espoused by the Prophet, etc. is incomplete. God can change anything, at any time, throughout history. God is doing that right now! Today's Revelations prove this. Revelation #15 is brilliant and so special for humanity and so very much needed today for both Islam and Christianity. (Possibly other religions also, yet this needs to be explored and discerned more clearly at this stage.) We must believe this, otherwise, we don't believe in the One true God of Eternity. *Too often we are not challenged to accept that God can do anything, anywhere, anytime, for any reason out of Love* *and Forgiveness, and* we should be challenged for God's sake that this becomes the aim and ideal in our world.

We Must Emphasise that -

NO VIOLENCE IS ALLOWED FROM HUMANITY BY GOD, IN RESPONSE TO THE NEW TRUTH FROM GOD TO THE AUTHOR.

Celebrate that Mahomad

Is Fully God and Fully Man.

Celebrate that Jesus Is

Fully God and Fully Man.

Celebrate that Islam and Christianity have much in Common.

Allah=Mahomad=God=Jesus

No Violence Allowed by God,

(Outside legitimate and reasonable levels of self-defense).

(Source, Revelation #15 to Bryan Foster 2016)

*Before **Heaven**: Hints Tips Stories*
Bryan Foster

Unique and Original Revelation #15

(See p. 107 for copy of the original transcription of #15 from God to Bryan.) When understood and enacted, this Revelation should promote God's religious institutional presence on this Earth, as the majority presence. One God Only for Everyone.

Today, around 55% of people are from the two largest institutional religions of Christianity and Islam. A much larger number is recorded when all others in the different religions openly accept the reality of God becoming human.

Because both Jesus and Mohamad were God Incarnate on Earth, there could be a high chance that other good, holy people have also been God Incarnate, or at least a prophet, in other eras and places geographically from other authentic religions worldwide.

It is a Revelation from God, which is the Truth, and needs to be acted upon now, truthfully, by the religious leaders of the mentioned religions, and other interested religions and parties.

Violence is rarely acceptable. Only in genuine self-defense, with appropriate, not excessive force.

This is a purely violence-free promulgation by our loving and absolutely peaceful God of ALL! Criminal and religious violence will show the evil of the perpetrators.

Anyone who concludes a need for violence BECAUSE OF Revelation #15 is so far away from what God wants from us!!!

This genuine, authentic – **Revelation #15 from God is real.**

Before **Heaven**: Hints Tips Stories
Bryan Foster

It is revealed to challenge us to develop a better more fulfilled truthful world for all, no matter their religion, lifestyle, career, beliefs, etc.

Any violence resulting from this Revelation by any people will be seen by God as EVIL, with the appropriate response eventually forthcoming from God. No religion will honestly need to encourage the evil of violence after reading and analysing this, Revelation. It is a beautiful Revelation for us all worldwide!

A few critical possible outcomes, which could help us all achieve full acceptance of this Revelation #15

- God can do anything, at any time, involving anyone or anything so chosen by God.

- God is divine and not physical, yet became Incarnate (physically fully human and fully God) twice in history - that we now know from these latest Revelations – God came as the Incarnate Jesus and *Mahomad

  (*This is God's spelling of *Mahomad within the Revelations, except once, when revealed to the author.)

- These Revelations were from God, through Jesus approximately 2000 years ago and Mahomad around 1400 years ago. Both Jesus and Mahomad were Incarnate of the one and only God of all time, of all people, of all religions.

- God loves all people equally and wants each person to eventually become one again with God both here and in

Heaven. Our response to God's absolute Love is what counts. If we freely choose against our known God, then what we do is evil. We do evil; God does not!!! God only Loves Fully!

- We have no right ever to challenge God about anything. We need to fully and absolutely understand and practise where we as humankind fit in this relationship. Good people are subservient to God always. Why? Because that's the best way to show absolute love for God. "Do with me what you need (Will), God."

- Many people find this imbalance too much of a challenge and go their own way - wrongly. Insolence is evil. People placing themselves equal to, or better than God, are evil – because they are going against God. That is what EVIL is! GOD = Absolute LOVE. Humanity is < God.

    Even though many people will be challenged considerably by *Revelation #15, we must react peacefully, and lovingly and explore what is being told about this Revelation. And how we can implement it as the Truth from our most Loving God.*

- God has advised that the religious leaderships, theologians, scriptural scholars, and others of the mainline monotheistic religions (and other genuine religions wishing to be involved) need to research quickly, pray, discern, etc. then explain and teach Revelation #15 and what is its impact, etc., on the world will be. Especially for the two religions directly involved, Christianity and Islam.

- Be it known and promulgated as quickly as possible, that: *accepting* **Revelation #15 will instigate an incredible wave of freedom and closeness with our God and each other** for all those open to God's latest, essential Revelations.

- This occurs because as a society, and not just as single religions, often disagree or even fight or argue with each other on various levels, usually on the divine religious, intellectual, spiritual, and physical levels.

We must listen to God's latest Revelations.

These Revelations are The Truth. These are true because God made it known that these were True Revelations passed on at God's direction.

Just as **Jesus is entirely accepted as God Incarnate for and by Christians, so must *Mahomad be also accepted as Allah/God Incarnate for and by Muslims.**

(* Mahomad spelled this way by God in the 2016's 15 Revelations, except for one time.)

*Mahomad now needs to be fully accepted by Muslims, as God/Allah Incarnate in Islam.

Allah=God=Mahomad

This is Allah's/God's main message for Muslims today, from Bryan Foster's - Revelation #15 from God - More detail in Book 5.

(Book 5, *Jesus and Mahomad are God,* 2020, Bryan Foster, Great Developments Publishers, Australia.)

Muslims please don't jump to negative conclusions and get stuck on *Mahomad only being a prophet and spelt this way.

Yes, this has been correctly taught, believed, and lived so since Mahomad was alive on Earth.

However, God recently updated this teaching even more. Mahomad is also much, much more than just a prophet. He is Allah/God.

That is, Mahomad is also God Incarnate.

Yes, fully a prophet, but now according to God/Allah, fully Allah God too.

A genuine scanned copy of the original handwritten Revelation #15, 2016, is on p.107.

Hell = Absolute Evil and Total Isolation

Knowing God, or much about God, but Choosing Evil Before and After Death – i.e., Rejecting God Outright – Most Likely Ends at Hell!

As we live throughout the decades of our lives, we are freely choosing good or bad (Love or Evil) constantly. This personal growth, over decades for most people, but obviously shorter times for those who die young, gets us to a stage within our lives to make that final decision at death. People move between various levels of both ending existences throughout their lives, depending on their lifestyles and choices made at various stages of their lives. Good or bad constantly becomes interesting depending on the individual's circumstances and abilities to choose to do Good (i.e., to choose God)

People aren't all aware that they have a last choice at the moment of death, based on their lifestyles of Love or Hate, and loving God, or knowing of, or about God, and even then, eventually rejecting God.

This option hasn't been shared too much from the known to the unknown within our world and our lives. They also need to understand and appreciate what is happening then and why it is happening. If God and Love is decided upon by the various individuals and these people are virtually 100% close to God, they will probably be close to entering Heaven. The choice wouldn't be too difficult for these people.

*Before **Heaven**: Hints Tips Stories*
Bryan Foster

If at that moment of death, the person knows of God and God's place within our world, and still chooses Evil and Hate, mostly based on their life experiences where they normally chose against God, for whatever reason, and *this Rejection of God places the person at the evil end of life, through their total rejection of God, then Hell most likely awaits them forever!*

Hell is only for those people who know and yet hate God and freely choose to Reject God. God makes the after-life decision for each person with each person.

Hell is not for all Atheists. Many atheists don't reject God out of their lack of knowledge of God. Hell is for those unrepentant sinners who rejected a known and understood God outright. *Hence, we don't fully know God's thoughts on who actually gets to Hell, all we know is that most of the rejectors who know of, or know God, are most likely going to Hell after death.* This is at the higher end of hate, but hate is pure evil. From our experiences of Good and Bad, Love and Hate, we know the differences for ourselves and for others on this Earth. Are we with God or against God, i.e., are we Lovers or Haters?

Just because a person doesn't like or love God, you must wonder why and how(?) this doesn't make them go to Hell. *God gives people so many chances to be in Heaven because this is the final ending, He desires this for everyone. Out of Absolute Divine Godly Love, God 'awaits' us all from Earth to choose and be in*

Heaven with everyone one and all of His creations. Yet, certain people will choose Evil on a grand scale, even with an informed understanding of God, for whatever reason they do, and because of this total and absolute rejection of God and God's Absolute Love of all His creation, human, flora, and fauna, they choose Hell!!!

Before **Heaven**: Hints Tips Stories
Bryan Foster

The common belief of humanity is that **those who are absolutely evil do exist and live their lives according to an evil ethical philosophy/morality.** *Others within society cannot believe such a belief happens and try to wonder why?* Unfortunately, most evil, hate-filled humans, live an evil hate-filled life, because it somehow suits them better than the alternatives. (For whatever reason they decide upon as chosen for their lifestyles.) Some people know of no other alternative, often because their families and friends they mix with are mostly evil, selfish, and hedonistic, and believe everyone should be like them. Yet, this in itself isn't a reason for Hell. *The reason for Hell is very specific and it comes down to knowing and appreciating God's existence, and then choosing out of hate to reject God and God's Absolute Love. You really must wonder; how does this happen? Why would people choose hell? Remember they can only go to Hell if they reject God and God's Absolute Love for all of God's creations, after knowing about these and much about God too.*

We would have to imagine that knowing this end game of Hell for those very Evil Rejectors of God, is a very true option. Basically, people who hate and Reject God outright, throughout their lives and life choices, show a real falling out by them from the grace and Love of God. Their choice ends up being Hell, after totally Rejecting the Absolutely Loving God and all that God does and stands for…

Our lifestyles while on Earth, dictate mostly where we will end up after death. Those who work towards Love as best as possible have earned their existence in Heaven. Oppositely, those who enjoyed a lifestyle of badness, wickedness, and evil, and wholeheartedly rejected God along the way, will have earned their place in hell after death, if their beliefs are still evil and who are still Rejecting God outright.

*Before **Heaven**: Hints Tips Stories*
Bryan Foster

Heaven or Hell?

At Death - The Choice Really Begins.

God gives us this one last choice when we die. So much will depend on our lives here on Earth. If we choose God throughout most of our lives, especially near death, we should be at an outstanding Loving place of mind and soul at that time of death.

Are you so in love with the One and Only God of eternity that you will choose God at death? God's Heaven or evil's Hell?!?! Our preparation while still living on Earth, helps so much at death.

Be at that state at death, whereby you:

Won't choose Evil and Hell!

Will choose God and Heaven!

I very much believe that I need to complete my God-given tasks firstly, i.e., Publish the 10 books; Pass these to as many religious leaders, scholars and theologians as possible. Develop the three Facebook groups and the two Blogs attached to the websites.

Hopefully, I will clear up this uncertainty about me being a prophet before long!

Before *Heaven*: Hints Tips Stories
Bryan Foster

God Aware and Informed Evil Rejectors most likely go to Hell.

*If we **reject a known** God and choose evil, hateful, anti-God decisions, we must suffer the consequences, whatever that may be as chosen by God.*

Having Absolute Love from God, we should always choose the right, good and Loving decisions for God. Do we though?

Forgiveness is given to us by God to be able to sort out the non-Godly choices and behaviors we choose to make with others, and ourselves. We similarly turn back to God through 'His' Loving Forgiveness, which God shares equally, as with Love, with all people.

Love needs forgiveness as part of the healing process.

DO KNOW GOD, but DON'T REJECT YOUR KNOWN GOD OUTRIGHT - as HELL AWAITS THOSE WHO DO (Total Isolation and Hate-filled.)

You may possibly not believe in God's existence or be unsure about God's existence, BUT **YOU MUST NEVER REJECT GOD OUTRIGHT and PERMANENTLY,** if you know of and about God, or believe in, God. *Rejection comes from those who know God or of God but deliberately choose against God – i.e., deliberately choose to REJECT God!!!*

If I said that I have communicated with God through receiving these various Revelations which God gave me, what would you say? If I claimed that these were passed to me in 2016, 2018, and 1982, 21+1 Revelations in total, how would you respond?

*Before **Heaven**: Hints Tips Stories*
Bryan Foster

If I claimed that these 10 books in the *'GOD Today' Series*, have the Revelations from God for Today, plus Discerned Divine Inspired Messages from God over decades, etc., would you agree it has to be possible, even though you have little or no idea of God's or the Revelation's existence?

Truly Rejecting God and God's reality and the Truths He shares is Evil. God who you know exists, after your death, brings forth your rejection choice, which is Hell after death.

Most people are loving individuals by their very nature. Most of these people have no idea how anyone could reject God and choose Hell on this Earth after their death. What must these rejecting God people believe for this to be a reality for them? It doesn't matter what they believe in instead of God. God is certainly real. No discussion is needed.

Most likely these non-believers, atheists, or unsure of God's existence people, agnostics, claim a belief of no Heaven or God, or Hell or evil. **This is not some 'undergrad. university debating society' or social justice issue discussion, where everyone is respectfully listened to and believed to a degree, if at all possible. And all beliefs should be accepted or at least respected, so that no one is made to be fully sad, upset, disappointed or maybe even hated(?) for their presence and different beliefs. Not knowing God, not loving God, not believing in God, etc., is NOT the same as Rejecting God.**

Hell is for those outrightly Rejecting their known God after death!!!

However, people have the right to honestly change their opinion for one last time, at or immediately after death. It is a discerned belief that if they find

*Before **Heaven**: Hints Tips Stories*
Bryan Foster

that extra special love, they may change their mind and choose God at or after their death. This then changes and they can then go to Heaven.

Even now God still has the last choice! If God chooses otherwise which I believe would be incredibly unlikely, yet still possible, you may not have had your sins forgiven. Something is probably holding your intention for forgiveness to not be fully forgiven by God!

However, common sense says that if your life is so antigod, pro-evil, hate-filled and rejector of God and most other good things of life, then you are more likely to go the same way at death – Evil – Hell!

Many of the world's population would thoroughly enjoy that you could engage in some fruitful discussion for the world to grow and become a most God-loving, people-loving, peaceful place forever. Unfortunately, I feel we'll have to wait quite some time before we can get a genuine, respectful loving discussion or lifestyle acceptance going through the rejectors – if ever actually?!

But we should never give up trying to bring the lost to be the found. It is one of the greatest gifts, offerings, and challenges of all from God, for us to encourage the non-believer to be prepared, and look forward to, going home to God, Heaven, and all other creations who made it there!

My most memorable experience of sharing some religious thoughts on social media was received exceptionally harshly, disrespectfully, and cruelly. These mostly self-proclaimed non-believing rejectors were quite spiteful, vindictive, and basically evil – everything against a belief in God was their aim for themselves and everyone else – that's evil, if understood, planned for, and enacted!

When your deliberate, hurtful attack/unfounded arguments dominate, mainly due to your evil vilification of God and God's believers, the non-believers' evil actions and beliefs enter the world and try to convert the God believers openly or covertly to atheism, or to rejectors of God. This point cannot be stressed enough. These non-believers, and/or rejectors of God, are trying to convince or force God's believers to their hate-filled beliefs and lifestyle – this action itself is pure evil when it outrightly rejects God, i.e., rejecting their known God outright, and the person commenting forcefully, is being evil personified. Many would argue that this isn't anywhere near evil! However, would not many have great difficulty explaining evil in the first place?

Yes, everyone has a right to their beliefs. *However, in this article, rejectors of God are being called out, because theirs is not a loving movement but in general an evil, hateful one! A free choice is taken to be away from the Absolute Love of God. Rejection of the One and Only known God is supreme Evil! Hell is supreme Evil. This is continually being highlighted here due to the possible evil outcome.*

To reiterate – with the earlier chair analogy. i.e., the chair you are sitting on is real, whether you believe it or not! You can yell as loudly as you can, huff and puff as much as you can, and scream that you have a right to your own personal opinion, as much as you can. Unfortunately, the result of this is not your case! **The chair is a chair no matter what!!! Hell is Hell no matter what! Heaven is Heaven no matter what! God is God, no matter what.** Free Will or your personal opinion can be totally varied from others. But if you don't believe in God or Heaven, that changes nothing. God has revealed thoroughly that God exists, that Heaven exists, that absolute love and forgiveness exist, that Free Will

Before **Heaven**: *Hints Tips Stories*
Bryan Foster

exists, always knowing that Free Will is sometimes just like your personal beliefs i.e., not true at this particular time. **Free Will is not God's Will.** *Free Will is our ability given by the Absolutely Loving God to have and express our own personal beliefs and opinions, whether correct or not!*

Can an atheist and/or rejector of other people live similarly to how a believer in God loves others? This depends so much on what level of rejection of God is believed by the atheist. *Total outright rejection of God by the atheist and others, moves those people so far away from God that very little, if any, love from God remains with them. Their love from God has gone through their evil choices. Humans' love goes freely, God's love can never go from God. When this evil diminishes the ability to love others is diminished, and a person becomes so hateful most often, that no loving relationship can be seriously formed, depthed, and lived. God is Absolute Love who loves all of us Absolutely and Equally, for Eternity. Evil sinners of varying degrees, freely move away from God.*

Just as nothing remains the same forever, **a weakening for some reason in the atheist's nonbelief of God, may be enough to encourage the atheist to reconsider God, God's perfect loving ways, and move to, or back to God.** Moving back considerably enough *hopefully* would end up with the atheist *moving from atheism to agnosticism to lover of people and hopefully then lover of God.* This is obviously one of the ideal solutions. And one possible course to take.

Yes, to God=Heaven! An outright rejection of a person's known God after death=Hell! These are discerned inspired messages based on various Revelations and IM) from God to me over many years.

Not believing in God or not sure about believing in God, the agnostic is on a search for God or for no God. This is not evil. It becomes Evil, when people outrightly Reject the one and only God of eternity, after knowing of God or God's

*Before **Heaven**: Hints Tips Stories*
Bryan Foster

existence, etc. **Rejection of God is the most harmful movement humans can engage in when linking our lives with a search for God and Love.**

Most of humanity are believers and will stay that way for their whole lives. Most of these believers will remain quiet, believing religion/spirituality is personal. They won't get dragged into uncomfortable debates, etc. Is it possible in this present time that responders who disagree with the contents of this book, be not so evil, hateful, and destructive??? My social media religious experience would profoundly challenge this desire for worldwide, loving peace. *There is way too much anger and hate out there in our digital world today, mostly directed at a supposed 'non-existent God' or the various institutions and leaderships worldwide.* Obviously, a very limited appreciation of the most wonderful God on High exists. We cannot ask people, unless Free Will exists for all people – which it does. From this comes the right to discover finding God themselves, or at least begin the personal and communal search for God.

Yet, I would very much welcome these rejector people to be open to offering their thoughts and beliefs, respectively, and listening carefully to the other side – the believers. But firstly, I strongly suggest that you are very open to God's options and prepared to go along with some or many of these.

This book is provided as an opportunity for non-believers, and unsure believers, to read about the Truth about God's existence and to explore relevant topics. God asked me to do this.

This isn't debatable in the vindictive way shown to me on social media. But as a crutch to find genuine, awesome Godly facts and emotions. Don't forget how this works…

Before *Heaven*: Hints Tips Stories
Bryan Foster

Unless evil people stop continually rejecting God and stop becoming absolute haters, deniers of Love, and outright rejectors of God, **they will never experience the powerful, genuine, true love God offers us all equally – including them.** There will be certain smaller atheistic, rejecting groups within larger atheistic groups of people who are stuck between a rock and Hell.

Mt Warning/Wollumbin <u>Word of God's Revelation</u> – the Background Story

In 2016 God 'came down' from the mountain. This majestic Australian 'mountain' in the Northern Rivers, NSW, offered forth a most remarkable experience of God for the author. Having just spent three days touring around Mt Warning, reflecting on it, photographing, and videoing it, and staying in a caravan/trailer park on its plain, all was to culminate in a nighttime oneness with God event. This Revelation moment is indelibly etched on my whole being.

I had the most remarkable opportunity to experience God's Word firsthand, literally. I had taken leave to recuperate from illness and stayed for a few days in a caravan in my wife's original hometown. The campsite I chose significantly had a view of Mt Warning in the background. A 'mountain' I had viewed thousands of times over the years, particularly since I was 18 and had met my future wife and her local farming family. Mt Warning is an imposing 'mountain' feature in the far north of New South Wales, Australia. I say mountain it really isn't in any comparative height-sense like the mountains of Europe/Asia or the Americas. For the oldest continent, Australia, it is quite imposing. Being a volcanic core, it stands out literally within the caldera features of a vast ancient volcano. The shape is very appealing and attractive. Its centrality within the region causes it to be a feature admired in all directions.

Over three days, I drove the 72km around its base and up to the walkers' departure point (on bitumen and gravel roads). Around sugar cane farms and through national parks and small villages, I videoed and photographed it from all possible directions, sat and reflected with it, observed it, drove, and walked to crucial observation points, visited its base, and became very familiar with it. You could almost say, I became one with it.

On the third day, I was awoken at night. I was very aware of my breathing and of breathing cold, fresh, clean air. I just lay there breathing deeply in through the nose, holding each breath for a couple of seconds and slowly blowing it out through the mouth. There was a real sense of presence. I started to realise it was quite a cold night and that I was lying at the foot of Mt Warning, in my caravan. I began to get this powerful awareness that I was one with the mountain. The mountain and I had grown together significantly these past three days, and now we were at a climax. The Truth would become apparent.

I then started to get a message to write down what I was about to receive. And to be very accurate. I soon began to realise that, just as in ancient times, the mountain was a conduit to God. Prophets from many religions had climbed mountains to be closer to God and to receive God's message for that time and place in history and often for subsequent eras. I was not to climb the mountain tonight. (Or ever again due to an injury.) But I was to climb it figuratively. Or was it a case of God coming down from the mountain?

*Before **Heaven**: Hints Tips Stories*
Bryan Foster

Remarkably, what followed blew me away! Without thinking about what I was to write, I found myself writing down a list of instructions, teachings, and refreshers. Was it truly from God? It sure felt like it. But how could I tell? I was told within my mind not to overthink this; to go with the flow - that it was all legitimate and would become apparent as the night went on. The challenge for me was that since my 25th birthday religious experience (See 25th birthday story in Appendix 4), tears were a sign for me of God's presence, the greater the tears, the greater the divine presence. (See 'Tears from God')

Yet, there were no tears tonight. But there was ecstasy and a realisation of what was happening. A font of wisdom was unfolding, and I was so, fortunately, a part of it. The list was completed. An explanation from me of what had occurred was recorded after the list. (See 'Revelation Notes' after the 'God's 12 Revelations' section.) And a perfect sleep followed.

The next morning was a Sunday, and I attended the Catholic sacrament/ritual of the Eucharist in the church in which Karen and I were married forty-four years ago this year! The mass was by coincidence a First Communion Mass for the local Catholic school. During the Mass, I asked God if what happened last night was real – what followed was an outpouring of tears. The answer was an emphatic, "Yes!

*Before **Heaven**: Hints Tips Stories*
Bryan Foster

Where it all began – Author's 25th Birthday

The day doubt disappeared, and my faith journey went to an unimagined higher level. On this day, I gained a whole new perspective on God and God's part in my life. Tears from God's love were experienced for the first time. The doubt about the reality of God disappeared. 'Let Go and Let God' became an actual spiritual reality of a profound order.

The stars all seemed to have aligned. It was my 25th birthday. As well as the school's uniquely offered, annual 'Commitment Day'. It was also my last day at this school. At the end of the day, I left this school for my first country school principalship – which began on the Monday after leaving Brisbane.

It started with birthday excitement but the last day of school sadness and ended in tears of absolute joy and oneness with God.

This school was unique in its philosophy and enrolment policy. One key difference to most schools was its strong association with the charismatic Catholic movement. This was especially manifested in the annual 'Commitment Day' to God. Various staff had special gifts from God, which they actively used within the charismatic movement, but are not limited to this movement. Many people have these multiple gifts from God but often aren't aware of such gifts. The other common one is Speaking in Tongues, which I have witnessed on many occasions. On this day, the seven teachers with the charismatic gift of healing were engaged for much of the time healing students and teachers alike. This healing encompasses any weaknesses we have, e.g., physical, emotional, or social.

*Before **Heaven**: Hints Tips Stories*
Bryan Foster

On this day the students and staff of this junior secondary Brisbane Catholic school began the day with a special Mass celebrated by a charismatic priest from Melbourne. The mass was followed by an invitation to students and staff to commit to God sometime throughout the day. There was no compulsion, though. The students could roam the school freely throughout the day with the only prerequisite being no noise near the church. Staff supervised.

The staff of fourteen had seven charismatic teachers who had the spiritual gift of healing. One of these, the principal, was a sister in a religious order. Throughout the day there were a number of these charismatic teachers, plus the priest, present at various positions within the church. Students could choose whom they would like to pray with when offering their commitment to God. Most stations would have many students continue with the staff member.

I sat with a particular student during the mass. This student was in a few of my classes. It took about an hour after mass concluded for this student to ask me to accompany her to pray with the principal and her present group of students. It was quite an event to go through the process to get there, due to various circumstances. However, once there, we were invited by the principal to move to the front of her group of eighteen to twenty students. Sister asked this student if she would like us to pray for her. She then asked me if I'd like to place my hand on the student's shoulder and pray. I agreed and prayed for her from very deep within my heart and soul - no speaking in tongues, just everyday English.

This belief in prayer causing healing, however, had caused me significant challenges that morning. I was tearing myself apart

Before **Heaven**: Hints Tips Stories
Bryan Foster

inside through the doubt that enveloped me about the whole healing circumstances that had been occurring in the church that past hour. Not being a charismatic person myself and having significant doubts about the entire healing process through a person being prayed over action, caused me major concerns. Much of this doubt was based on the television evangelists we would see on Sunday morning television back in the 1970s and 1980s where people were miraculously 'healed' in large numbers before our very eyes as if this was the norm. There was truth to many of these healings, yet there was always so much doubt, as well. It was remembered that many of these tele-evangelists eventually admitted to fraud or other inappropriate behaviours. I had also witnessed charismatic healing at a local Brisbane parish while eighteen years of age and at a teachers' college. This impressed me enough to want to consider it more. The tele-evangelists over the previous years up until this Commitment Day made belief in this healing process very difficult indeed.

So, as I walked this young lady to Sister, I was in incredible anguish internally. I was fighting against the possibility of something incredible. Each group had people who were crying or sniffling, and all were arm-in-arm with each other. It seemed to be too much for this doubter. Once I was asked by Sister to pray for the young lady, I instantly decided to 'Let Go and Let God'. This freeing moment was something quite unbelievable. The confusion and doubt turned to belief and love. Sister then placed her hands on the girl's head and prayed. At that moment, the student broke down and tears freely flowed. I was now also tear-filled.

Next Sister asked if I'd like her to pray over me. What followed was life-changing. As she placed her hands on my head and prayed, there was this incredible feeling of heat flowing from my head downwards to my feet. I then broke down and cried tears of absolute love for God and those around me. This is the moment in time when all my confusion, doubts, and challenges about God disappeared.

Later that afternoon, I asked Sister what had happened, and she explained that it was God who came into me and that my old self was 'washed away' (downwards), and that I was 'filled up' with the new me.

I have remained so faith-filled and full of God's oneness and awe ever since – that is 36 years. My faith has never wavered since that day; even when some very challenging issues have confronted me. God was with me through each of these.

That was the day I truly learned that tears in specific instances are a sign from God - that God is truly present at that moment.

I am often asked if a similar experience of how God came to me, along with the Tears from God, will happen to others, to my former students, their families and friends, my colleagues, etc. I genuinely believe that it could if the opportunity availed itself. We need to accept God's offer, whenever and wherever made. We may need to search out the possibilities. We may not expect it when it does happen. I believe the secret is always to be open to receiving God in both expected and unexpected ways. God loves us beyond our imagining and wants the best for each of us. We must not be blinded to God by all the distractions of this world. We need to be prepared for God to come in whatever way God chooses. It may not be what we expect, though.

We need to clear our minds and hearts to the beauty, purity, and awesomeness that is God. We need stillness, openness, and desire to accept whatever God offers, whenever God provides it.

The notion in much of the Western world today is that we don't need God. It is either because we have so much or because we are blinded by so much - which is an absolute fallacy.

We need God as much today if not more as in any time and at any place in history have needed God. It is the first significant time in history that the belief in God and acceptance of God being with us on this earth is diminishing. It is a time of absolute urgency requiring a major cultural shift towards the One and Only God and God's people here today.

Islam, Christianity, Secularism – Today's Key Challenges

Islam and Christianity

'Jesus and Mahomad are God' highlight God's desire for the world's two largest religions to be thoughtfully and respectively challenged to become more wholesome and loving institutions and communities for their followers and others worldwide. And to include these latest two Revelations #6 and #15 in their teachings, etc. This is all about genuine LOVE from God for each other, no matter religion, denomination, or culture.

Islam and Christianity need to accept the challenges and move forward significantly. In this case, based on the Revelations and inspired messages, the author has received from God and explored in this *'God Today' Series* of seven/eight books.

*Before **Heaven**: Hints Tips Stories*
Bryan Foster

It is now time for the followers of Islam to realise that no one is threatening them with these new additional Revelations and messages from God. They will need to accept that it is not just very probable for God to do this, but that God has done this!

In fact, not just very possible but well within the expectations of many of their followers no doubt. People of this world are calling out very loudly for Islam to accept more Revelation and inspired messages from God.

Secular Challenge

Secularism is dangerous and hollow! It lacks any substantial depth and belief foundations. It is based on not needing the spiritual world, the world of God, and God Himself! It believes humanity is the only strength and power needed for a successful world. That all answers lie within the human spirit and entity.

How far from the truth could this be? For anyone who has experienced God in their lives directly or indirectly, this is a sad joke. In all honesty, who hasn't experienced God in nature, in goodness (Godness), in prayer or meditation, in other people through what they have said or done which has had a major impact on them, etc. Some of these experiences may not show God intrinsically, yet particularly when a person is open to these experiences, God will become seen. Many people will have direct experiences with God, where they know in their heart of hearts that God has just made direct contact. This may happen through any of the experiences listed above. However, God does give people direct knowledge of God's presence through 'tears from God'. Tears confirm some message from God. Tears flow and God's actual presence is truly felt.

Secularism is leading humanity to a catastrophe. Firstly, the valued, historical, worldly institutions start to crumble. Respect is lost. The individual becomes the centre of the universe. Broad, accepting communities unravel. Nationalism, communism, narcissism, nihilism, and totalitarianism, along with many other 'isms', flourish. Already our communities are crumbling. Look at the racism and police killings in the USA, the growing racism and anti-Church/God growth in Australia and Europe, etc.

The lack of respect or even contempt is shown to our politicians and the political class. The growing lack of respect for the law and police. The hate-filled reaction to the Church, Islam, and other anti-religious/God sentiments growing today. When respect for groups, institutions, and religions within our society dies, our society dies! The answer is found in God's teachings through various genuine religions, prayer, religious experiences, etc. **God is the answer – not the problem!** Listen to God's messages, God's people, and your personal experiences of God.

It is God's Choice

There is nothing wrong with this notion. God does not stay still. Neither must we. As the world grows, develops, and changes very regularly these decades, so too must we be prepared for God's religious developments to be genuine and necessary. God/Allah calls Muslims through modern-day religious laypeople, one example being this book's author, to listen very carefully to the latest Revelations and messages from God. God has said these things in the urgency of hope to the Islamic followers of God.

*Before **Heaven**: Hints Tips Stories*
Bryan Foster

Muslims are not being forced or coerced into anything they don't need, but they are being challenged to search out what it is that God commands from Islam and for Islam in today's world of continuous and significant changes. Allah/God is calling for Love, Peace, and Acceptance of all genuine religions.

The number one idea is to promote worldwide theologically, that no more violence or death can be metered out by any religion or culture, especially in this case of fundamental religious followers from various faiths. Muslims must accept that taking significant steps forward and not living in the 6th century, or any other era up unto the present time is essential for a satisfied, happy, and non-divided world – a world of love and not hate!!! A society existing for all people, of all faiths and cultures equally. A beautifully supported world from the one and only God forever! An exceptional existence will then be created for followers of Islam and all other religions who aim to benefit from these latest Revelations. Listen to the world of various religions and denominations. Hear what they say. Adapt this to your beliefs and actions. Be well-informed about the Qur'an and be accurate in disseminating its teachings. Don't exaggerate any teachings that males of the warrior age (i.e., the teens, twenties to thirties) would find incredibly enticing. Include these new Revelations discussed in this Book as being from God for all Muslims and Christians, and all other people living today. Quote the Qur'an honestly, without exaggeration or truth-stretching. Be open to the Truths stated by Allah/God.

Allah/God loves ALL people within this world now, previously, and forever, equally! No matter their differences or to which religion each belongs. Genuinely following the one true God of all creation and of all time should be the aim of all religions today!!! God always loves us equally. It is we who choose to either not love God or various people.

Islamic followers grow into the massive new light that awaits you from Allah/God!!! The world is ready and wants you as part of its fully functioning and legitimate beliefs and practices to become one with all the other religions and cultures. Not to be fighting these other genuine religions and cultures.

The violent Islamic fundamentalists, e.g., ISIS, and all others who profess violence from any faith, along with individual secular groups and deniers of God, must STOP NOW!!! God demands!!! It is violence against various groups, Islamic and otherwise, and subjugation of women's, children's, and many disadvantaged rights, and all peoples' equality with men, which are some of the main disagreements. The extreme fundamentalist Muslims' violence against other Muslims and their denominations, as well as other religions, is out of the misunderstood God who makes it very clear in all genuine religions that all people are equal no matter their financial 'successes', social standing, career, gender, religious leadership, etc. It is the people who turn away from God through their sinning, not God turning away from the people. God never turns from people – because God is absolute LOVE.

The vast majority of peaceful Muslims and their leaders, along with our political world leaders, must stop the violent followers of Islam (and any other violently passionate religious people from any other religion). It is a difficult task, yet an essential one for world peace. It is something everyone needs to support and act on in their own best ways.

There is only ONE GOD for all religions, for all cultures, for all genders, and overall time! The One God appeared to various cultures, whenever God wanted to, for whatever reason God wanted, whenever God wanted to do so. No one or religion has any right to claim God as their own and ignore everyone else! God, the one and only, is for everyone in whatever way God desires. For all genuine religions, God is the only God – forever, past, present, and future. If this is still not how God is seen, then it is their duty and obligation to change now at God's instruction. This Revelation, to us, should have a significant impact on all religions worldwide. No one's God is better than anyone else's because there is Only One God for everyone, every religion, every generation, every culture, and every person throughout history for eternity. There is no competition. There is Only ONE GOD for everyone, forever. (** There are not multiple gods for each religion, just the One and Only God for everyone, for of all time.)

The secular world and those following secular philosophies are being urgently called by God to refocus on God and God's supporting Revelations once again. Don't be ruled by fools-gold – be ruled by the absolutely ONE and ONLY God… Just as Islam needs some radical changes and development to move successfully into a modern-day Islam, so do many of those predominantly coming from Western-secular societies.

Their God of importance worth following is a heretical stance by these secularists, who basically know about our one true God, but refuse to be lovingly engaged with God. It is also evil! Choosing anything but God and moving voluntarily away from God is evil! Yes, everyone has the personal option to believe in and follow God. Free Will is essential for loving choices – no force, pressure, bullying, etc. Those who know very little about God and live their lives in kind, considerate and loving ways, are innocent in God's eyes. However, those who do know of God and have various genuine beliefs about God, but are denying God, are genuinely evil and moving away from God while on Earth. Their choice at death would most likely be a continuation of their earthly lifestyle, i.e., moving towards or being at, the evil state of existence. This would then progress in death as in life – a permanent evil presence and not a Heavenly, loving one, unless the person sort genuine, authentic forgiveness from God and was truly sorry for all their evil.

'God Today' Series – Brief Overview from 10 Books

1 God ONLY!!! Forever. For everyone. Transition Now.

Should be Only 1 Religion - Transition Now

All people are Equal. People choose to sin and move away from God. God wants all people to go Home to Heaven. Forgiveness of all sins, particularly grave ones, is essential.

*Mahomad and Jesus are both God Incarnate i.e., Fully God and Fully Human. 4 000 000 000 of the 8 000 000 000 people on Earth are probably God Incarnate, i.e., one God Incarnate for each Human alive. (Details of this, on immediately following pages.)

Unique Images caused by the sun support God's messages and Revelations for us. Tears from God and sun arrows and crosses, etc. are real. Both sets are to help us find, believe, and live fully with God.

Love is the Meaning of Life. Especially - God's Absolute Love!!! There is also Love from a secular perspective too.

*Before **Heaven**: Hints Tips Stories*
Bryan Foster

21+1 Revelations received by a lay person, the author, show God communicates and sends Revelations and Inspired Messages to many of Us - Not just clergy, religious sisters and brothers, theologians, religion scholars, religious leaders, etc.!

ALL LIVING CREATIONS, humans, fauna, and flora from God, have a high chance of reaching Heaven and God. Soul=Life. Probably inert objects created by God may too.

Know God. Know about God's teachings, etc. and Reject God at death – Hell awaits.

(*Mahomad as spelled each time (except once) by God in the Revelations in 2016.)

Before **Heaven**: *Hints Tips Stories*
Bryan Foster

Is it True?

Did God send me this in December, 2022 ????????

I came across this most, MAJESTIC, INCREDIBLY, POWERFUL MESSAGE, FROM GOD, BUT IN QUITE A STRANGE WAY!

You are invited to work through this, just as I need to do, so as to come to a closure with a decision, (R), (IM) or neither? At this stage, for me, it hasn't been accepted as the Truth.

SO MASSIVE.

SO CHALLENGING.

SO GOD.

*Before **Heaven**: Hints Tips Stories*
Bryan Foster

(If it is True!?)

>>>>>>>>>>>>>>>>>>>>>>>>>>

>>>>>>

ONE or TWO UNIQUE and POSSIBLY VERY SPECIAL MESSAGES FROM GOD? Dec. 2022 and Jan. 2023?

Is this supposed to reveal #A (next page) as

1. Revelation? or
2. Discerned Inspired Message? or
3. Neither (Dec. 2022) – REAL? (see p.110)

You are Invited to be seriously Challenged by this possible Revelation from God.

It is MASSIVE in its CONTENT, CONTEXT and UNIQUENESS, and will be a very real challenge for most of Us!

#A = GOD'S INCARNATION TODAY (R), (IM) OR NEITHER. 2022, Dec.???

#B = ONLY ONE RELIGION FOR ALL. Transitioning now. (IM) 2023, Jan.

#C = ONLY ONE GOD FOR EVERYONE FOR ETERNITY (R) 2016, May.

"One God Only One GOD" Revelation #10, 2016.

#A and #B - Two New Revelations, or Two Inspired Messages or one Revelation and One Inspired Message or Neither?

Revelations or Inspired Messages for this next article. #A is incredibly complex – unclear to the author still, as to whether #A is a Revelation or a Discerned Inspired Message or Neither. Reflections, Prayer, Discussions continue.

> A. Each Second Person is God Incarnate for each Human. Known or Unknown by the Human. Many details from God are lacking at this stage. (R) or (IM) or neither?

B. There Needs to be **Only One Religion** for All People for Eternity. (IM)

C. There is One and Only One God of All People and all God's living Creations: people, other fauna and flora creations, for Eternity, past, present and future. (R)

Two New Revelations or Inspired Messages (or neither) from God. #A. 2022 (29, December) + #B. 2023 (7, January.).

The author received one new Revelation (R) or Inspired Message (IM) or 'something else' from God on 29/12/2022 and another one on 07/01/2023. The background to these promulgations by God is explained here. I would very much like to invite you, the reader, to hopefully experience something of what I have been receiving over the past seven years. This is incredibly significant and, no doubt, will require considerable time and acceptance by humanity overall. Is it too much 'out there', too complex, or too challenging, for most people? I hope not. I certainly initially found it a challenge, and still do, to a degree.

The discussion following occurs in the chronological order of the understanding development of these two (2022 and 2023) (R) or (IM) or not, for me. **Hopefully, it helps you the reader, and others you might know who are interested in such articles, to see how various times the author's thoughts, beliefs, and challenges progressed.**

Revelation or Inspired Message or something else/neither? #A - Each second person within our world will be God Incarnate for one other human being. *Due to the different way, I received it, compared to the other Revelations I received over the years, I am not certain of it being a Revelation or a Discerned Inspired Message or? But it could be one of these two options, due to the Tears from God received during and after the YouTube song by Collabro (see next page), along with when I shared this experience through the numerous thoughts and discussion points, with Karen, my wife.*

At this moment, my thoughts are more favouring a Discerned Inspired Message. Mainly because God never asked me to write down the Revelation, as with most of the previous Revelations from God, (except the 1982 Revelation at Seton College). Hence, 1982 (R) referred to as the +1 in the Revelations stated as 21+1, in my writings, and #A in 2022, are similarly presented by God. But this doesn't discount it being either (R) or (IM) or other possibilities.

If this teaching from God is real, this (R) Revelation or (IM) Inspired Message says that each person alive will have a God/Human Incarnate partner. This God Incarnate Person can move around, when directed by God, to other individuals worldwide throughout the individual's life. It isn't necessarily just one specific God Incarnate for each person's lifetime.

*Before **Heaven**: Hints Tips Stories*
Bryan Foster

Receiving Latest Revelation or Inspired Message now #A = 21+(2) if this is a Revelation. But would still be 21+1 if it was an (IM) or something else.

After viewing a YouTube song sung on Britain's Got Talent from 2014 for **Callabro's audition, (they eventually won the BGT 2014 title), I was suddenly receiving a possible Revelation of a different kind from my other (22) from God - yet this was spiritually and emotionally as strong and real as previously experienced when receiving Revelations. This began with four of the singers turning unrehearsed and very naturally inwards towards the fifth young man singer in the center of the group of five, when the words **'God be my witness'** were sung (*'Stars'* song, from *Les Misérables*). **All were smiling or reacting in a very special Loving, Godly, informed way. The special words, beautiful singing voices, genuine empathy, etc. were close to overwhelming. God was truly present.**

It is very powerful, but is it a Revelation? Or a Discerned Inspired Message? Or neither? Or something else?

Source -

** Collabro Britain's Got Talent 2014 Winners! | ALL PERFORMANCES - YouTube)

** Collabro 2014 - Google Search

God then said to me, through my spiritual, divine reflective thoughts from the One and Only God forever,

"You know that I want every human being to end up Home in Heaven, if at all possible." Followed by the astounding, "4 000 000 000 people on Earth today are being supported by another 4 000 000 000 God Incarnate people." (Quotes were written as recalled briefly after these experiences with God on Dec. 29, 2022, and Jan. 2023.) This means that literally half of the Earth's population are everyday people, and the other half are God's Incarnate people. Or maybe angels' or even prophets' Incarnates? Somehow? But a possibly incredible gift from God for all of humanity; being one on one or 50/50, God Incarnate and Us.

I am still working through this. (How are you reader feeling here?)

Those five young men should/could be a massive new reality from God for each of us. *God also called me, and most likely, many others worldwide, to help lead us all to a most extraordinary, divine reality.* If this is God's choice?

Part of God's most incredible <u>possible plan</u> for His Absolute Love of all people comes down to a very surprising 50:50, 1 on 1, reality of the God of Salvation through His Incarnated self for each human. This will surprise most people, I believe. I am still very surprised!

This unique aspect of God's plan seems to me to be leaning more toward a discerned (IM), due to its uniqueness as an Inspired Message, as never before mentioned or taught by God, for us.

Another supporting argument is that it follows the theme of Revelation #15 from 2016. Already we have two Incarnations of God, according to Revelations from Him in 2016, that Jesus and Mahomad are both God Incarnate. See page 137 for Revelation #15, received by me during a night in May, 2016. It became the theme and title of Book 5, *Jesus and Mahomad are God*.

***From another viewpoint, it could quite happily be a Revelation, due to both its uniqueness and its brilliance and majesty, as something only God could do, which also brings us along with Him, searching for Salvation and needing certain divine directions and guidance.*

God's Absolute Love and Forgiveness for each of us is so incredibly strong that **He has given us the absolutely best chance possible of going home to Heaven with Him through this new Absolutely Loving, Encultured, Compassionate and Forgiving Revelation or (IM), if it is fully true?**

A One on One, 50:50 opportunity, for everyone! That's Absolutely True LOVE!

Every move could be assisted if we want it. No excuses for not getting to Heaven now. This Absolute Love and Forgiveness etc. of God for each of us is experienced through the Absolute assistance of each of our Incarnate God/s, if this is the actual reality so desired by God?

The world is in a most difficult place today, and God often doesn't get a 'foot in' from many others worldwide. *He may have created this most incredible 50:50 opportunity for everyone, no matter whom they may be, and whether it is an (R) or an (IM) or something else entirely. This isn't necessarily important.*

Of course, we can freely refuse to accept or reject this! This is our decision, which could affect us or the consequences from our actions.

If it's true, you would have to be such an evil person not to see this Godly offer is legitimate for what it is – Salvation in Heaven with the Absolutely Loving God of Eternity.

Let Go and Let God Do It!

It's your Call and God's Delivery!

Don't forget the One-on-One assistance we may utilize here on Earth, after possibly being received freely from God if we want it.

Could be, 1 Human + 1 God Incarnate per person = **An exceptionally high level of guidance with the massive chance of being with God in Heaven.** (We must live God's plans exceptionally well.)

If it is a true (R) or (IM), then each second person is God Incarnate - *i.e., fully God and fully human, as God has hopefully revealed to me, and presumably, to many others.* You the reader too? This is the same reality that has occurred with the Incarnate Jesus and the Incarnate Mahomad.

Angels and Prophets?

This appears to make the role of angels and prophets different now, if God leads the way with His Incarnate chosen people/God.

Without yet receiving the details that religious scholars and theologians need for their complete reflective and prayerful analysis, etc., there is much yet to receive, analyse and implement worldwide throughout all legitimate religions. Along with any other people or groups that God so decides to invite.

Before **Heaven**: *Hints Tips Stories*
Bryan Foster

Of course, God may have informed the previously mentioned religious academics and leaders independently of me and others.

Possibly the angels are God Incarnate or God's Incarnate assistants for various humans and maybe even some sort of divine trainers/educators? Along with the angels are the human prophets. This group of people will likely help guide us with/to/how as needed with our incarnate Saviour/s.

We could imagine statistically (if this concept is used by angels, etc.?) that each angel and prophet would be highly needed these days to help get this whole (IM) or (R) of 50:50 God Incarnate reality understood, and truly appreciated by all people. This following explanation will truly challenge many of us or set the reality firmly with all these Incarnate God(s) within our world.

Out of the world's 8 billion people, 4 billion would be God Incarnate, as so far understood from the new (IM) or (R) if true. This is just so incredible and shows an Absolutely Loving God of all creations, time, people, and places, etc. Alternatively, as seen above, **what many people believe are possible angels or prophets, may in fact be God Incarnate people, angels, or prophets, etc.?**

What better source of divine guidance could we get than from a personal God Incarnate reality? Once we realise this, how could we ever freely choose to sin again? Specially to sin gravely?!

If anything, it may be too different from what people are expecting.

As God revealed to me, God's (IM) or (R) is very much based on getting people Home to Heaven with God.

What is being claimed here is very different from what we and others have probably expected from God and have previously been given to us from God!

God so much NEEDS us to do what He wants, out of His Absolute Love for each of us, so that we can all be saved and go Home to Heaven with God.

Knowing this, we must do as asked by God, and choose the divinely inspired lifestyle wherever possible. The billions of Incarnate Gods would come from the One and Only God of eternity. How? God can do anything God so chooses. Except sin, which He would obviously not do! Sinning is rejecting God! By definition, and Absolute Love, this is not possible for God.

God can't reject God! God loves us so massively that God doesn't want us to miss out on Heaven. This teaching from God is a virtual salvation method. It ties us in to the strong possibility of choosing to do exactly as God desires from us. This is done freely by us through God's Absolute Love and Free Will and our Informed Conscience given to us personally by God.

Having a Divine God Incarnate with us, is a sign of God so much Loving us, that it seems almost impossible to not be saved and go to God in Heaven! Yet even so, we still must use our Free Will and Informed Conscience to make the correct decisions with God.

This 1 on 1 / 50:50 God Incarnate, truly shows God's Absolute Love for all His creations, and absolute Need for them all to be saved!

As a somewhat familiar reflective statement goes, God Loves our world and humanity so much that he came to Earth to experience it! Obviously, this is mainly a spiritual statement as God can do anything, anytime, anyplace for any perfect reason. If this statement is anything like true, then according to this latest (R) or (IM) or something else (neither?), then God is directly experiencing this in the billions all the time being half of the incarnate God, until He probably decides its end time for it, or everything universal.

These statements and descriptions are our human way of understanding and appreciating something so difficult to fathom at any human level. God as us now, being incarnated, fully God and fully human, also now knows our levels and how we react to God. In divine understanding I believe that everything we do, describe, believe, apologise for, etc. has already been planned, done and may develop into something else or even start again. But we still must work our way through everything we face, faced or will face again.

The difference between God and Us is phenomenally different. Divine God – Basic Human.

Hence, God's all-out assistance for everyone's Salvation with God in Heaven has been offered to Us all. As is always the case with God, humanity is responsible for making the correct decisions lifelong. Using our Free Will and Informed Conscience, we can all choose God's requests for each of us, or not!

The MASSIVENESS of this TEACHING from God, only matches its UNIQUENESS.

This is truly exceptional and for most, I feel, like myself, mind-boggling, if TRUE!

How could we ignore the Incarnate God,

being fully God and fully human,

being next to us throughout our lives and then us committing a hurtful or even one of the gravest of all sins,

knowing what we will then know about God's Absolute Love and Forgiveness,

and our deeper wisdom from God about Good and Bad choices!?

This will become apparent if we can accept that this new #A Revelation or (IM) is real and true from God,

if that is now, or in the future?

If this is true and ready for dissemination (if ever),

it will be a critical and unexpected (R) or (IM).

Yet it may be neither, but still from God to Us,

from the Absolutely Loving God of Eternity.

*Before **Heaven**: Hints Tips Stories*
Bryan Foster

HAVING ABSOLUTE LOVE BY OUR SIDES IS ABSOLUTELY PHENOMENAL.

It very much shows how God so much wants each of us to go to Him in Heaven at our deaths.

If this is true, each Incarnate God option helps our trajectory to our Divine Heavenly Home to become so real and achievable.

We may or may not know which is our God Incarnate person/spirit. The workings of this Revelation or Inspired Message or (?) haven't been told to us or the religious leaders worldwide, yet. God will clarify this whole teaching sometime in our future.

The Incarnate God/s worldwide can help positively change people they guide regularly, as our relationships, needs, wisdom, love, etc., changes over our lifetimes? **This is all, so that, if possible, all humanity eventually returns Home to God in Heaven.**

Author's role? My role is to introduce God's Revelations, to get these out to as many people as possible. Especially to various religions' scholars, theologians, leaders, clergy, etc., in Christianity and Islam initially. And further afield as time goes on… (now if other religions see the huge benefit of this possibility for them).

At this stage, the author still feels this is leaning towards most likely being an Inspired Message more than a Revelation, God's Truth being developed over time within the author and others. **Even though its receival method was quite different and it seems incredible, but almost massively way too big to be an Inspired Message (if size plays any part?), than a Revelation???**

But then, why not??? God can do anything!!! Even so, I am feeling more comfortable for it to be a Discerned Inspired Message? Trust in God fully!

The Truth will set us Free!

However, we need some level of proof to confirm it is from God e.g. for the author there are the Tears from God; along with photographic images of the sun and cloud formations, as has occurred to the author a few times; and also various coincidences, etc. (See Book 4 in this Series for unique and original and spectacular images from God.) These are common methods I've experienced over the years.

If it is from God, consider how very important this is for humanity and the world?!

Receiving latest Revelation #C = 21+(2?).
Received by Bryan Foster on 07/01/2023. (Previous 21+2. Now + 1 = 21+2 Revelations.)

Today, **#B, 2023**, is believed to be an (IM). #B had already been discerned as an **Inspired Message** (IM) to the author from God many years ago. **#B. There needs to be just One Authentic Religion Overall for all people, for all time.** All genuine religions need to become One Religion.

(Revelation #C, received 2016) Creation is ruled by the One and Only God of Eternity, for all the People and God's Living Creations Worldwide or Universe wide forever.

Previous 2016 REVELATION #C Especially Needed Today. *The religions that exist worldwide now, should worship the One and Only God forever, as per the 2016 Revelations.* However, during the transition, all religions could also remain who they are, accept the same One and Only God for all religions, and move to interpret, analyse, reflect, etc., while developing their own wisdom for the unification of all religions into One Religion under the One and Only God of eternity. I now feel more passionately that #A is an (IM). Time helps all (IM) become clearer and will help my appreciation of this #A being either an (IM) or possibly even a Revelation. Hopefully much more than just, something else!

If fairly implemented by each religion, this should result in each authentic religion becoming stronger, especially as there is now no reason to object to, or harm, any other religion, its beliefs, and practices, etc., or any person/s within those religions, as should have always been the case. Each religion should grow stronger and closer to each other. Moving closer to becoming One religion Only, with the One and Only God of Eternity!

Before **Heaven**: Hints Tips Stories
Bryan Foster

'Revelation' or 'Inspired Message' #A is Complex,

and in its raw state, maybe well beyond many of us, being quite difficult to appreciate? How each legitimate religion's religious and scriptural scholars, academics, theologians, leaders, etc., pray, reflect, discern, and explore it, I imagine, will take considerable time, prayer, debate, and consensus, etc.

It is up to us, if we have genuine Godly Love, Forgiveness, Compassion, etc., to assist in whatever way is possible, each and every person we are able to, who may be in need of assistance. Humanity needs to assist people with various needs, everywhere.

Whether Revelation or Inspired Message or neither, of #A, isn't the whole answer? Our assistance from God, is incredibly outstanding, and is always phenomenal.

If a true reality, is so much Love from God, it is very difficult for us at this stage to comprehend and apply it to our lives fully. Yet, we must try with our new God Incarnate 'partner'. Includes the author's opinions at this stage, after a lot more clarification, reflection, prayer, discussion, and life's lived religious experiences.

True or False?

Genuine, Massive, Revelation or Inspired Message from God? #A? Or nothing, but a possible misread by me of God's message to us.

> Is it a Massive Revelation or Inspired Message or Nothing? You would not have believed it – but it is right there from God in December 2022. A most spectacular, hugely personal, and I would imagine it could possibly be an indirect highly, supportive ending, for this *'GOD Today' Series*, no matter what it is or isn't. Where could it actually take us in the future?

For this Most Incredible teaching from God, there are several serious challenges to its authenticity. Beginning with the style God uses for me to receive various teachings from Him. As you will see, if not already, God's Revelations to me, except one, have come during the early morning hours around 3am on two occasions, when awoken by God in 2016 and 2018. The one difference was a Revelation received through a special high school 'Commitment to God' day in Brisbane in 1982, when I was prayed over by the school's charismatic religious sister principal.

Tears from God came, as well as a most beautiful warmth that flowed internally from the top of my head, where sister's hands were placed for praying for me, down to my toes.

It was also my 25th birthday and my last day at this secondary school before moving my whole family that afternoon to a small primary school at Tara, in southern Queensland, to be its new principal.

Hence, this shows that this possible new Revelation, may be a true Revelation, with God using a different method to advise me of it. God can literally do anything God so wishes, except be evil. The answer is still unknown, as we search, reflect, pray, for the correct answer.

Continued in Book 10…

Before *Heaven*: Hints Tips Stories
Bryan Foster

GOD Today' Series – 10 Books' Overviews

The Meaning of Life is Love. God's Love

Book 1. *1GOD.world: One GOD for All* (2016) introduced in detail the first major Revelation from GOD in 2016 and challenged the reader to search and find GOD through other people, nature, and GOD's Revelations (R) and Inspired Messages (IM). It introduced the author to the reader and shared twenty-six of his personal, spiritual, finding-GOD, 'everyday' stories, hopefully encouraging and assisting others in seeking and finding GOD. A series of inspired messages discerned by the author over his lifetime was shared.
OUT NOW

Book 2. *Mt Warning GOD's Revelation: Photobook Companion to '1GOD.world'* (2017) is a 72-kilometre photographic exploration around Mt Warning/Wollumbin and up to the walking track's starting point. These were taken over three years, culminating with the Revelations from GOD on the plains at the foot of the mountain one cold winter's night in May, 2016. It is a photographic and short story of the spectacular and spiritually inspiring Mt Warning and its surrounding towns, landscapes, and fauna. Images are taken from most angles around its 72km base drive, plus the road up to the walking track. This book provides a physical feel for the Mt Warning region where so much of this *Series* was introduced or occurred. **OUT NOW**

Book 3. *Where's GOD? Revelations Today* (2018) invites the reader to continue the journey of exploring who and where GOD is for them and what are GOD's messages for today's world. It details twelve Revelations from GOD for today, received within the Mt Warning, (Wollumbin N.P.) region. A collection of another six Inspired Messages received within that same 24-hour Revelation period is shared. A key focus is on assisting the reader in their appreciation, understanding, and searches for GOD in today's world. Bryan's photographic images from God, through God's use of the sun, clouds, rainbows (and a moonrise – Book 6's cover image) and other landforms, leads to some UNIQUE and SPECTACULAR images that are shown in the supporting photobook in detail. Book 4. These are explained in this Book 3. **OUT NOW**

Book 4. *Where's GOD? Revelations Today Photobook Companion: GOD Signs* (2018) surprises the reader, as well as the author initially, with some exceptionally SPECTACULAR, UNIQUE, photographic images, some possibly formed by God from various reflections and refractions of the Sun, or as the author believes, more likely given directly to humanity from GOD. Some sun arrows and sun flares were formed across the author, along with spectacular sunshine shapes created in the sky. **Especially look carefully throughout the book, within the images presented for sun-formed arrows, flares, a huge Easter sun cross, double rainbows, and cloud formations.** The initial images occurred at venues on the plains of, and at the foot of, Mt Warning/Wollumbin N.P. Shortly later, these types of images were also given by God at Cabarita and Kingscliff beaches, in the northern NSW Rivers, and at Cylinder Beach, North Stradbroke Island. And a UNIQUE giant Easter sun cross was seen inland in Texas on the Queensland/New South Wales border. It is believed to be one of its kind anywhere. Another sun arrow was seen across the author at Vernon in British

Before **Heaven**: Hints Tips Stories
Bryan Foster

Columbia, Canada. The Sun is central for many people to imagine and discern GOD and GOD's beyond-our-reality extraordinary powers. Other spectacular sunrise and sunset images are shared. The author strongly believes each image from God is sent to encourage and inspire the author to develop this 10 book Series, based on God's Revelation, Inspired Messages, Key Points, and Images, that God has shared with him and others worldwide. Our Sun is the centre of our world – no sun, no lives. Overall, these genuinely spectacular and MOSTLY UNIQUE pictures say thousands of words combined. These pictures tell a 'thousand words'. **Author's Favourite. UNIQUE, SPECTACULAR, AUTHENTIC PHOTOS.** **The photos are so genuinely STRIKING and UNIQUE, that Book 4 is the author's favourite Book of this Series.** ***OUT NOW***

Book 5. ***Jesus and *Mahomad are GOD*** (2020) (Revelation #15, 2016). A massive challenge for around fifty percent of the world's population is issued by God. Both Jesus and Mahomad are the Incarnate One and Only GOD. Each is fully God and fully human. Revelation #15 is this Book's title. Prayer and relationships with GOD and the Incarnate GOD hold critical possibilities for our future world. The first and possibly overawing Revelation that is the basis for this Book, came during the Revelations from GOD to the author in May 2016. The world will be religiously challenged like possibly no other time in history. The extremists and the violent must remain faithful and peaceful, no matter their likely strong desire to do otherwise. No excuse! Our loving, most peaceful GOD allows for nothing else. **GOD won't accept any violence, especially in 'His' name, and for such an Absolutely Truthful and Necessary Divine Revelation!** One essential outcome

Before *Heaven*: Hints Tips Stories
Bryan Foster

becomes the divine example of GOD's Love – we are all equal and holy before GOD - until we sin and by choice freely move away from God. Forgiveness from us is then required to move back closer to God and others affected. A most profound and exemplary reality of GOD is the Incarnations of Jesus and Mahomad at different times and places in history. See the original handwritten original Rev. #15 on various pages within this book, for example, p.78. (*Mahomad is spelled this way, except for once, by God in the 2016 Revelations.)
OUT NOW

Book 6. *Love is The Meaning of Life: GOD'S Love* (2021). A significant exploration of what Love is and how it affects us all, introduces this Book and is the theme followed throughout. There is a substantial discussion on the types of Love, its positive impacts, and sometimes challenging impacts, and how we can grow in true Love throughout our lifetimes with our special loved ones, family, friends, colleagues, communities, and of course, with GOD. GOD is seen as the Absolute Lover in His Perfection. God loves us all equally and desires absolutely our perfect union on this Earth and ultimately with GOD in Heaven. GOD's Love and People's Love are explored in detail. A most enjoyable, shared experience of one person's lifetime with God living in today's world. The author is very experienced with God, Religion, schools, families, parishes, and the local deanery... Bryan Foster taught in religious schools for 42 years, including 30 years teaching the Study of Religion to Years 11 and 12 students. He was a primary school principal twice, and a secondary school's assistant principal of Religious Education (+ pastoral care and administration) for 12 years. He was also both a parish and a deanery pastoral council chair and secretary. This book includes many of these life experiences, which hopefully

will encourage others to search in similar ways to those explored in this book. A refreshing read commented by many.
OUT NOW

Book 7. Wisdom: GOD's Hints and Tips (Author Articles) (2021) A book of Wisdom from GOD to the author, which I believe has been seen as something special by our readers. GOD is sharing some outstanding essential beliefs and lifestyle messages. So many Revelations, Inspired Messages, and Vital Loving information from GOD to today's people are shared. It is a unique encounter with some refreshingly insightful Wisdom quotes, including some challenging ones, as well. The first group of extracts from the three collections, i.e., firstly Revelations, will range across the reader's lifetime and are linked as examples to that stage of life. The bulk comes from the first 60 years of a person's life. The author is the example used here to help us understand and appreciate where we are with God today. How these can help each of us, no matter our age or maturity, will be the reader's challenge, and need some genuine support, as we progress through life. People who especially enjoy spiritual and human reflections will be drawn to many of the quotes. The second group is the 21 Revelations to the author in 2016 and 2018. At the same time, the third group contains the highlighted Inspired GODly Messages found in each book within this *Series*. Each one encourages serious reflection and addition to our lexicon. The author developed these with GOD's perfect influence and written over the past 40 years. These should add and support each reader's quotes from God. Then shared with others as felt appropriate. **OUT NOW**

Book 8. (8A and 8B) *Love is The Meaning of Life (2nd ed)* (2022). This second edition of (Book 6) *Love is The Meaning of Life: God's Love (2021)* is *a secular approach, without the considerable*

emphasis on GOD as is shown in Book 6, the first edition book. *8A is mostly secular*, with limited mention of God or Religions, etc. Book 8A is followed at the near 2/3s of this book with Book 8B. This book has some different special topics linked to both books 8A and 8B. It is also that the language and discussions will be clear and non-complex. Hopefully, without the often-found necessity by various writers to make it so convoluted. Doing so often leads to losing the level of appreciation by the reader of the topic of Love. Yet, *because GOD is a perfect Love and needed for any deep loving relationship, there is a limited but necessary discussion on this point in 8B, i.e., in the last 1/3 of the book.* The author did not minimise GOD's Truth in any edition of these books. An accurate story/explanation of what Love is and its impact on our lives is explored. People often get confused when speaking of Love, as there are several types and levels of Love, which impact us all to various degrees. GOD is Absolute Love. Love is what we are trying to gain continually throughout our lives – no matter what our understanding of Love is to each of us! Circumstances change, and so do relationships. When we achieve the true Love, we also gain God! *It is a book on Love for all people. You might enjoy seeing where this may lead you, with or without your belief in God, over as many years as you would like to reflect on it.*
OUT NOW

Book 9 alternative. The previously advised photobook has been changed. I felt a need to explain some difficult and/or challenging themes and issues within the last two books in this Series, Books 9 and 10.

Book 9. *Before Heaven: Hints Tips Stories* (2023)

Book 9 introduces some difficult themes covered within these last two Books 9 and 10. These will be added to, theme and depth-wise, in these last two books of this Series. Various Revelations (R) and discerned Inspired Messages (IM) will be developed in this Book 9. The main theme explored, which is still a major challenge for me, will possibly 'blow your mind away', or at least challenge you to reconsider so much of our surrounding creation, and the place of people. Is it actually True and sent from God? Much more reflecting, praying + significant scholarly input and theology, is needed. See this Book 9 for considerable details. In this case, we will be including Incarnated God/people, (note 'people', not 'person'), i.e., people in huge numbers – 4 000 000 000 and sent from God worldwide. Book 5 developed the fact that God asked, during His Revelations to me, to write down all He said to me that 3am night in May 2016, while I was camping near Mt Warning/Wollumbin, NSW, Australia. God revealed that both Jesus and *Mahomad are God Incarnate i.e., fully God and fully human. God sent me two (R)s or (IM)s? (Unsure at this stage, which type though was the first one, #A, when I was completing this Book 9 recently.) At this stage, without further proof, the first one, i.e., #A, will be classified as an Inspired Message (IM). As for all (IMs) time will tell as each of these IMs develop through God to me, and I would assume others worldwide. Another serious *Before Heaven* issue is understanding Hell and choosing the best methods needed to go to Heaven and not Hell.

The biggest challenge we have for this Series, is the authenticity of the teachings of two possible major Revelations sent in December, 2022 and January, 2023, supposedly from God and discussed in this Book 9. These seem very genuine, yet the method of receival by me leaves some doubt, when seen next to the normal way that I have received Revelations, IMs, or (neither?) before. Only time will tell. Yet, some doubt it still occurs. Depending on how this processing of the major theme goes, about half of the population should now be Incarnated Gods. This finding goes before or after publication for me. It will have an impact, to some degree, on this possible Revelation, before these points are accepted as authentic and genuine. If it is necessary and the level of this Revelation #A is seen as of the Revelation standard, after publication, this will be discussed and corrected in Book 10 later in 2023. **OUT NOW**

Book 10 *Before Heaven* – Hints Tips Stories (2nd ed) (2023) This latest and last book of the '*God Today' Series*, aims to bring the themes and challenges of the ten-book series together, based on and including God's Revelations and Inspired Messages and my experiences with God. The 2022 Message from God may significantly impact this last book. Only time will tell after much reflection, prayer and hopefully sharing with religious leaders. If it does offer a strong appreciation or explanation of its progress, this will be given. We should be aiming to get as many of the Revelations (R) and Inspired Messages (IM) from God, into each of our Earthly minds, hearts, bodies, and souls. To then ask all of us to assist with passing these on to as many people as possible in today's world and to the world of the future. *This book uses many stories, from various sources of mine, linked to the theme being covered and written in a non-confusing manner. Hopefully 'Keeping it Simple', as directed by God back in 2016.*

Book 10 contains 180+ pages of various types of short stories, Revelations, Inspired Messages from God, Answers to various questions asked of the author, etc., – all assisting the leading potentially to our successful return to our Heavenly Home with God. These are based on many of my experiences in growing to becoming very close and hopefully One with the One God of

*Before **Heaven**: Hints Tips Stories*
Bryan Foster

eternity; an aim, I believe, we should all consider very seriously. Some may be quite challenging, but all should be enjoyable, depending on where the reader is in their life's journey. The inclusions are primarily based on the themes and topics covered throughout the *Series*. This is along with original and new content and strong links to necessary topics and approaches throughout it. The approach used included highlighting key points from the previous nine books, including the two photobooks, showing how these aided others and me in discovering God, Love, and Life, and the closeness we should have with God. Special themes include God, Incarnations, Love, Heaven, Life, Angels, Prophets, Evil, and Hell. Many prophets, along with God's Incarnations, of Jesus and *Mahomad, are known by many of us through this *Series*, and our lives. Each scriptural input, collected by the prophets and the 'Holy Men and Women' of various religions, will assist us to find God's answers in our lives, in everyday happenings. These include the good, angelic, and divine, and the bad and evil, of life. My final view, at this stage, of the massive number of incarnated people discussed and introduced in Book 9 will be shared. 4 000 000 000 people may be incarnations with God?
OUT 2023

(* Mahomad is spelled this way by God in the 2016's 15 Revelations, except for once.)

Conclusion

God has so much incredible impact on those eventually discovering and believing that there is a God. And then who act upon this brilliant wisdom, knowledge and understanding, that they are discovering and learning about. **Our One God of All Forever has Absolute Love for all His people, Equally**. Being Absolute Love, God doesn't have bits of love different for each of His creations. Our God with us now, has been the One and Only God forever in the past, and will also be there forever to come. God and Heaven are with us Always, just as each has already been the case up until this stage in the universe. Our Only One God forever, is Absolutely Divine, Absolutely Loving, Absolutely Compassionate and Absolutely Forgiving to each of us, as we are Absolutely Equal for God. God will do so much for each of us out of His Absolute Love for us individually. All living creations come from the One and Only God of Eternity. This would be the same for other creations wherever these may be within or outside our own universe.

God's first command overall for today's world, is to accept lovingly, that there is only One God for Eternity past and **Only One Religion for all of eternity** to come. That One Religion will be a combined One worked out by the leaders of as many of the genuine religions already existing, and probably others unaffiliated with any popular religion. God commands us to Love all people equally, just as done by God for each one of us individually and equally. This also goes with our reaction to those who have chosen evil; however, if there is a possibility of harm to ourselves from the evil ones, we can try to change their evil ways if we so believe it is possible and safe here on Earth. If we believe that we can't do this safely, then we need to move away from them and their influence on us. We need to be careful about our own health and protection. Children need to be extremely careful and protected from evil people. Best to keep away from evil. Book 1 has considerably more detail on these topics, in line with the books' themes within this *Series*.

Where do we go from here, with so much already given to us by God? Do we pretend that we know it all? Of course not! Do we move forward as a people ready for our destiny?

The ten books in the '*God Today*' Series, hopefully will add considerably to the lexicon of the divine and physical worlds, becoming one with the Divine God challenging the religions, beliefs, worshipping and emotional ways etc. within the religious aspects of the world of today.

By now we have heard so much about the new parameters of God's worldly presence, or lack of, in various communities, that our first question must be, where is God now? Who really does love God beyond anything else, and shows it through their daily lifestyles, ethical choices, and outright love for those within their loving worldly existence? How do we know? Who's going to incorporate the divine with the physical world? Does God really give us a say in our lifestyles, religious beliefs, various earthly freedoms, etc.? Yes, God does, wholeheartedly! But do we honestly believe so and **how far are we prepared to go with God on everything? That's the massive challenge for all of creation – Absolute Love, Forgiveness, and Compassion, with God at the centre of everything!**

The Revelations (R) from God to us all through our received Revelations in 1982 (1), 2016 (15), and 2018 (6), challenged us all to grow so much closer to God and each other person we meet, through our Love, Honesty, Lack of

*Before **Heaven**: Hints Tips Stories*
Bryan Foster

Greed, Equality of Humanity, etc., as clearly listed in the Revelations sent to the author in 2016 and 2018 and physically experiencing God, initially in 1982, during Seton College's 'Commitment to God' day in Brisbane, Australia. This was when the religious charismatic sister, Catholic secondary school principal, prayed over me, and a beautiful warmth flowed internally from the head top, where Sr Ann's healing hands were placed, to my feet. This divine warmth and Tears from God occurred together.

Through my over 50+ years of closeness to God on Earth, particularly professionally through Catholic schools (and Catholic Parishes and Deanery) as a leader and teacher for 42 years, **comes my total belief and support of God's gifts to all people. I studied for Tertiary degrees at the ACU**, i.e., Australian Catholic University's campuses in Sydney and Brisbane, with a **Master's degree in religious education**. Professionally, I am so honoured to have had such a shared influence with my students. Many students openly accepted the challenge and worked towards discovering God and then living with God through each one's incredible Love for God and one another within our communities and society. Along with **my authentic Oneness with God, and hope for all others to join me**, has been my working together with the local Catholic churches, including through the leadership roles of **President and Secretary at the local Deanery and Parishes' pastoral council associations, and my children's school's Parents and Friends Association**. I was involved with these Church lay leadership associations for many years.

God's Inspired Messages, have been received and personally taken on board and taught, exemplified, etc. throughout our communities, parishes, and schools. I would have received over

100 (IMs), which I discerned to be very genuine and real, during these past 50 years. With my whole life now close to being in the same direction as God, I find that **the more open we all are to God and God's messages, the closer we become to a Oneness with God. We begin to live our lives with God being the central entity.**

The closer to God we get, the more of Heaven we begin to discover while still on Earth. Our Love grows closer to God's Absolute Love. As does our forgiveness and compassion, likewise. The Divine God becomes more and more one with each of us, through our prayer, life-long positive and Truthful Ethics, Love, Forgiveness, Empathy, and Compassion for all.

One (IM) stands out so much that it needs its own special coverage. **All creations from God, humans, other fauna, and flora, have equal opportunities to go to Heaven with each other, depending upon their Love for all creations, and lack of known evil within their lives. And surprisingly, God's created inert objects may also be included here. How this works for animals, plants and inert creations of God is unknown.** Except we need to grow in our beliefs that these creations are real, and at least have some level of intelligence and emotion, according to our limited human appreciation of such behaviours. For animals, how often have you experienced or seen certain loving reactions with humanity or amongst themselves? These are some of the most popular, publicly available videos on YouTube.

What if aliens were real also? My wife's and my two personal experiences, as will be shared in book 10, will possibly have challenged each reader previously, it certainly challenged us. But could it, in fact, be so real? Having a massive universe that is still expanding hugely since its creation, challenges us to seriously consider the reality and type of lifeforms in other galaxies and universes, on other universal creations, planets, stars/suns, asteroids, etc. **If these probable UFO travellers exist, they were created by God, as all lifeforms and creations are! Soul=Life – for humanity, at least.**

Total rejection of God at death, or after death, by someone who knows and understands God, leads that person most likely to Hell forever. *A world becoming quite secular is going to be challenged by God to repent and Love God and all of our communities more than anything else ever!!! God seriously wants every living creature of His creation, to be with Him in Heaven. All creation has that one last true chance for repentance – at that death moment with God.* If a person genuinely asked God before death for absolute and genuine forgiveness, and yet changed his/her mind after death, the after-death rejection of God most likely places these people in Hell – forever! Hell is a solitary, super-evil existence without God and any other living creation forever for each individual there. It is total isolation within Hell and for each entity existing in Hell, whoever these might be.

Revelation #15 from 2016, is so different from what people expect now, that it also needs special attention and explanations. Book 5 concentrates on this, being such a necessity within this Series, as well as it being that book's title, *Jesus and Mahomad are God.* **God became Incarnate, i.e., fully God and fully human, in Jesus and Mahomad (R)! Different eras and religions, but both very real and authentic.**

The major challenge comes from the two most recent 'Revelations / Inspired Messages'(?) from Dec. 2022 and Jan.

Before **Heaven**: Hints Tips Stories
Bryan Foster

2023. **Is it possible for 50% of the earth's population, 4 000 000 000 of the 8 000 000 000, to all be God Incarnate, i.e., fully God and fully human and linked by God with a specific person, or people, on Earth now and forever?**

How considerably helpful this would be for those humans having an Incarnate God? To make correct decisions towards being One with God and all of God's creations, forever. Imagine the possible amount and depth of Love surrounding each person in this circumstance. How close must God be to each of these highly supported people?

God wants all people in Heaven. Wouldn't this latest (IM), which I am leaning more toward it being this at this stage, than it is a Revelation, being truly open to Heaven for so many more through God's direct help for each person, through the partnered, incarnated other human? How challenges, beliefs, and realities associated with the possible 4 billion God Incarnates develop from now until Book 10 is completed before publication, will be explained, and shared worldwide, especially with my readers. Book 10 will complete, where possible, our understanding of the two new teachings from God, sent in 2022 and 2023. This image below **is the exact 15ᵗʰ Revelation from God to us all**. I wrote exactly as it was stated to me by God. It occurred in May 2016, when I was awoken by God **and asked to transcribe His Revelations exactly as God 'spoke' it to me**, while I was camping on the plains of Mt Warning/Wollumbin, northern NSW, Australia. I received 15

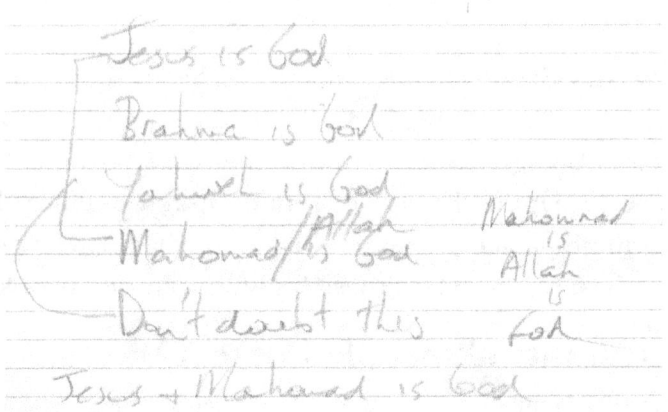

Revelations, which were written very accurately, as God instructed. #15 is below. **Different ways of approaching Heaven and ours and others' God-Given lives, while still alive on Earth, and before going home to Heaven, have been presented throughout this book.**

Some special inclusions are listed: There is the author's special 21+(1 or 2?) Revelations from God in 1982, 2016, 2018, (2022/3?); plus, a sixteen 'special combination by the author' of these Revelations and Inspired Messages from God. Some personal stories, e.g., medical issues and their impact on me, and hopefully somewhat similar impact to some of yours, the reader? **Physical evidence from God, such as Tears from God and Unique images, starting with the sun, with God creating images for me with sun arrows,**

Before ***Heaven***: *Hints Tips Stories*
Bryan Foster

sun flares, sun rays; along with a giant Easter sun cross outside Texas on the Qld/NSW border and photographed on the NSW side, are seriously worth considering while deciding on God's place in each of our lives. Book 4 has a considerable number of UNIQUE images from God. Many people worldwide have been moving away from God for quite some time now and are probably amongst the secular and/or atheistic groups.

Many of humanity believe in aliens and UFOs due to sightings, etc. Karen and I together have seen genuine UFO images taken by military planes in Australia, along with a freak experience in front of a television station's major antenna, next to its studio on Mt Coot-tha, in Brisbane and observed from Coronation Drive next to the Brisbane River in Queensland. **The divine invitation to be a prophet for God was made in the 15 Revelations paper from 2016.** It was separated from the other Revelations in written style and positioning. **It is still not fully decided either way. However, I am leaning strongly towards a 'Yes'.** More details are coming.

Books 9 and 10 challenge us in various positive and sincere ways in our relationships with God and humanity. One aim is to help us select the necessary information to help our lives on Earth be of a higher quality than the normal everyday lifestyle could be. Yet, we should have God's Revelations strongly included. **No debating about the accuracy of God's True Revelations. These are fully and absolutely the Truth, being directly from God. And revealed to me, and no doubt others worldwide, by God.** God only allows discussions, explorations, education, and support of His Revelations to

Before **Heaven**: *Hints Tips Stories*
Bryan Foster

Today's World! God's Revelations are divine, real, and needed today! *We can't challenge God!*

Bibliography

Primary source:

GOD's Revelations (R) Transcribed by the Author

Discerned Inspired Messages (IM) from God to Author and recorded in writing.

Secondary Sources:

Books, Videos, and Internet websites

Al-Islam, (2022), Books on Islam, Muslims, Prophet Muhammad(s), Ahlul BayAl-Islam.org

Ali, Ayaan Hirsi, (2016), *Heretic: Why Islam Needs a Reformation Now*, Harper Collins, New York.

Books 1-10. (Following). Foster, Bryan W., (2016-2023), *'God Today' Series*, Great Developments Publishers, Gold Coast Australia.

Book 1. Foster, Bryan W., (2016), *1God.world: One God for All*, Great Developments Publishers, Gold Coast, Australia.

*Before **Heaven**: Hints Tips Stories*
Bryan Foster

Book 2. Foster, Bryan W., (2017), *Mt Warning God's Revelation: Photobook Companion to '1God.world* Great Developments Publishers, Gold Coast, Australia.

Book 3. Foster, Bryan W., (2018), *Where's God? Revelations Today,* Great Developments Publishers, Gold Coast, Australia.

Book 4. Foster, Bryan W., (2018), *Where's God? Revelations Today Photobook Companion: God Signs,* Great Developments Publishers, Gold Coast, Australia.

Book 5. Foster, Bryan W., (2020), *Jesus and Mahomad are God,* Great Developments Publishers, Gold Coast, Australia.

Book 6. Foster, Bryan W., (2021), *Love is the Meaning of Life: God's Love, (2nd ed),* Great Developments Publishers, Gold Coast, Australia.

Book 7. Foster, Bryan W., (2021), *Wisdom: GOD's Hints and Tips,* Great Developments Publishers, Gold Coast, Australia.

Book 8. Foster, Bryan W., (2022), *Love is the Meaning of Life,* Great Developments Publishers, Gold Coast, Australia.

Book 9. Foster, Bryan W., (2023), *Before Heaven: Major Challenges from God (1st ed).* Great Developments Publishers, Gold Coast, Australia.

Book 10. Foster, Bryan W., (2023) *Before Heaven: Hints Tips Stories, (2nd ed),* Great Developments Publishers, Gold Coast, Australia. (Draft)

Foster, B., YouTube videos created between 2009-2023 – efozz1 (780+ Free videos at this stage. Changes will be advised.)

*Before **Heaven**: Hints Tips Stories*
Bryan Foster

Nolan, A., (2007), *Jesus Today: A Spirituality of Radical Freedom*, Orbis Books, New York.

Websites

An Introduction to Discernment
https://plenarycouncil.catholic.org.au/listening-and-discernment/

https://www.vox.com/2014/12/13/7382911/pope-francis-animals-heaven

Bartunek, Fr J., 2015, What is the Gift of Tears'?'
https://spiritualdirection.com/2015/01/26/what-is-the-gift-of-tears

Brahman - Gods or goddesses
https://www.bbc.co.uk/religion/religions/hinduism/beliefs/intro_1.shtml

https://www.bbc.co.uk/religion/religions/buddhism/ataglance/glance.shtml (17/11/2009)

Collabro Britain's Got Talent 2014 Winners! | ALL PERFORMANCES - YouTube

https://www.medicalnewstoday.com/articles/coronavirus-vaccine

Crusades, Christianity
https://www.britannica.com/event/Crusades

Fenelong, M, (2016) Receiving the 'gift of tears' in Our Sunday Visitor, https://osvnews.com/2016/08/23/receiving-the-gift-of-tears/

*Before **Heaven**: Hints Tips Stories*
Bryan Foster

http://www.greatdevelopmentspublishers.com/ - Publisher's new webpage. (Original website started in 2007, closed 12/2018.)

https://www.facebook.com/groups/389602698051426/ - 1God.world

https://au.linkedin.com/in/bryanfoster

https://twitter.com/1Godworld1 - Twitter

https://www.instagram.com/ - Instagram (1godworld)

Foster, B., https://www.bryanfosterauthor.com/

Foster, B., https://www.godtodayseries.com/

GCSE BBC, ttp://www.bbc.co.uk/schools/gcsebitesize/rs/god/chrevelationrev1.shtml

God Today, Facebook Group
https://www.facebook.com/groups/389602698051426/

https://www.ncronline.org/blogs/peace-pulpit/everyday-prophets-are-our-midst (2020)

Islam: Truth or Myth? https://www.bible.ca/islam/islam-history.htm

Judaism and Numbers
https://www.myjewishlearning.com/article/judaism-numbers/
Tim Muldoon, Author at Ignatian Spirituality. National Catholic Reporter. https://www.ncronline.org/blogs/peace-pulpit/everyday-prophets-are-our-midst

*Before **Heaven**: Hints Tips Stories*
Bryan Foster

Oxford Scholarship Online, Jesus the Fullness of Revelation, http://www.oxfordscholarship.com/view/10.1093/acprof:oso/9780199605569.001.0001/acprof-9780199605569-chapter5

Rattner, R, The Emotion of Devotion – Crying for God, https://sillysutras.com/the-emotion-devotion-crying-for-god/

Taylor, F, (2016), Life after death: What did Jesus do between his resurrection and ascension? https://www.christiantoday.com/article/life.after.death.what.did.jesus.do.between.his.resurrection.and.ascension/82998.htm

'Tears from God…' video at https://www.youtube.com/watch?v=z5mmNvIKko4

The Everyday Prophets are in Our Midst https://www.ncronline.org/blogs/peace-pulpit/everyday-prophets-are-our-midst.

What is the significance of the number 40 in Judaism? https://www.quora.com/What-is-the-significance-of-the-number-40-in-Judaism What is the Significance of Number Forty in Islam? https://salamislam.com/lifestyle/what-significance-number-forty-islam.

Before *Heaven: Hints Tips Stories*
Bryan Foster

Contents-Detailed

God Today Series x10 Books + Videos	7
Dedication	10
Contents - Brief	11
Contents - Detailed	185
Images	12
Foreword	14
Preface	15
Introduction	21
Highlighted Themes Explored	31

1 God Only Forever

Author Overview	36
Author's Credibility	36
One God One Religion	38
Christianity, Islam, Hinduism, Judaism on there being Only 1 God for everyone, forever!	39
Religious Commentators' Views on 1 God on Forever	43

Author and Prophet?

God asked if I would be One of His Prophets Includes, "I am prophet prophets are true"	45

Physical Evidence of God

1. Bryan received 21+1 Revelations. 21 after being awoken at 3am; once in 2016, another in 2018. 2. Tears from God. 3. Many Unique Sun Images from God. Coincidences.	50
'Tears from God' – Physical Proof from God	52
God-given Unique Sun Signs Attract Us	63
Sun Images Challenge Us	63
Book 4 -Photobook of God Signs. Many Unique Images	64

Before **Heaven**: *Hints Tips Stories*
Bryan Foster

Other UNIQUE Photographic Images from God

Sun Signs/Images Unique and Brilliant	64
Sun Easter Cross – Unique at Texas Qld	67
God-Given Unique Sun Signs Attract Us – Stunning…	69
Sun Images – Different Effects – Sun Arrows, Sun Cros	72
Book 4 (photobook) – Author's Favourite - UNIQUE	73

Unique Images Draw Us Closer to God	75
Book 4 Photobook – Author's Favourite	76

(See Bk 4 for extra special unique and spectacular images)

Challenges at Death and Just After Death

'Heaven' on Earth with God's Love	77
Challenges at Death and After Death – be very ready!	79
Humans, Plants and Animals (and probably inert creations) – can go to Heaven	82

Medical Issues for Comparisons?

Author's Medical Issues – possible starting point for shared experiences…	86
Necessary Medical Treatment ASAP	94
Medical Disclaimer	95

God's Absolute Love and Truth

God is Primary Bibliographical Source for *'God Today' Series*	97
God's Truth to Us + Evidence	98
God's Absolute Love for All Creation	100

Jesus and Mahomad are God Incarnate

Rev #15 from 2016. Muslims should now acknowledge Mahomad is a prophet and is God	101
Christians have always had Jesus as a prophet and God	102
God's 21+1 Revelations to Us in 1982 (1), 2016 (15) and	103

*Before **Heaven**: Hints Tips Stories*
Bryan Foster

2018 (6). Plus Inspired Messages over decades for author "I am a Prophet. Prophets are True"	103
Jesus and Mahomad Two Incarnations of God – Details	106
This Series is the first worldwide publication of Rev #15. No Violence. Original handwritten transcription by author from God, included for authenticity and credibility.	107 / 109
Unique and Original #15 Transcription from God to Bryan	112
Revelation #15 – a few Critical Outcomes from God	113
Islam Must Celebrate Mahomad's Incarnation as God/Man/ Prophet	116

Hell and Evil

Hell = Absolute Evil and Total Isolation for Ever	117
Heaven or Hell? God-Informed-Rejectors, go to Hell	120
Do Know God, but don't reject your known God Outright as Hell Awaits those that do	121
Mt Warning/Wollumbin Word of God's Revelation – the Background Story	127
Where it all began – Author's 25th Birthday	130

The Secular Challenge

Islam, Christianity, Secularism – Today's Key Challenges	134
Islam and Christianity	134
Secularism Challenge	135
It's God's Choice	136
'God Today' Series – Brief Overview of *Series*	140

Before **Heaven**: Hints Tips Stories
Bryan Foster

God's 4 000 000 000 out of 8 000 000 000 Incarnations

SO MASSIVE. SO CHALLENGING. SO GOD. 142

TWO New Revelations or Inspired Messages
from God. 29, Dec 2022. 7, January 2023.   144
Receiving Latest Revelation or Inspired Message –
now #A=21+(2)   145
The MASSIVENESS of this TEACHING from God,
only matches its UNIQUENESS - #A, #B, #C.   155
Having Absolute Love by Our Sides is a Phenomenal 157
#B Only One Authentic Religion Overall is Needed
for all People   159
#C There is Only One God of Eternity for All People
and Creation   159
#A Is Complex.   160

True or False (R)? (IM)? Neither? Answer yet?   161
10 Series' Books' Detailed Overviews   163

Conclusion   172

Some special inclusions   178
Bibliography   180
Contents Detailed   185
Key Summaries for Each of the 10 Books.   189
God's Gifts to Us + Our Responsibility in Return   191
Author's 22 Most Significant (R)s and (IM)s   193
Beauty, God and Us   201
God. Angels. Feathers - An Overview   210

Before *Heaven*: Hints Tips Stories
Bryan Foster

Author's Publications – Series, Books, Websites, Videos   212
Author's Websites   215
Overview of Author, Bryan Foster   216
Publishers   218

Key Summaries for Each Book

God Today' Series - 10 Books

1. One God Only Forever. Need to Move Towards: One God, One Religion, One Leadership, Scholars, and Theological Groups to be on the same page. One Main Set of Beliefs for all – i.e., one religion only for all people.

2. Mt Warning/Wollumbin. 72km Circuit - Photos of this author's Sacred Mountain, and from Various Angles. Plus, Surrounding Images of Mt Warning/Wollumbin, for Clarity of the Region. (Photobook)

3. Background to God and How we Get the Messages for Today. Key Revelations from God. God, Love, Life and Death, Science, Suffering, and major Reformations. God's sun signs to the author help the reader and the author believe and do as God requested.

4. Photographic Signs from God. Most key signs are UNIQUE and Spectacular. Began at and around Mt Warning/Wollumbin in 2018. Sun was the Main Source from God – giant sun cross, sun flares, sun rays, sun arrows. (Photobook)

5. Jesus and Mahomad are both God Incarnate i.e., Fully God and Fully Human. Existed in Different Eras and Countries. Revelation #15, 2016, is the most detailed Revelation from God out of the 21+1 (or +2) Received by the Author.

6. God's Love is Absolute and for Everyone Equally. What is Love from God? Challenges of Love. Solutions for Love's Difficulties. God's Special Loving Gifts for Us. Power of Forgiveness for All.

7. Introduction to Wisdom Quotes. Further discussion on the 21 Revelations along with the Inspired Messages from God. Key Messages and Wisdom Quotes from Books 1-6 further detailed.

    Exploration of the Background to the Key Points is detailed in the Appendices.

8. Introduction to Secular Love. Summative continuation of God's Love. Discerned Truths from God to Author. Linkage between both forms of Love. Book 8 Divided into Books 8A (Secular Love) and 8B (God's Love). Helps with comparisons of both.

9. *Before Heaven: Hints Tips Stories*
    Book 9 explores some difficult themes covered within these last two Books 9 and 10. The Book 9 discussion will be added to, theme and depth-wise, in the last book of this Series, Book 10. Various (R) Revelations and discerned (IM) Inspired Messages will be developed in this book. The main theme explored, which is still a

major challenge for me, will possibly 'blow your mind away', or at least challenge you to reconsider so much of our surrounding creation, and the place of people, including *Incarnated God/people* – the major challenging theme. At this stage, without further required proof, the first MASSIVE one #A will possibly be classified as an Inspired Message (IM). As for all (IMs), time will tell as each of these IMs develop through God to me, and I would assume others worldwide. It could still be a Revelation. Cont. in Bk 10, if needed.

10. *Before **Heaven**: Hints Tips Stories* (2nd ed)

The Author and Truths; God's Contact with the Author; Hell, and Atheists Who Reject God Outright; Heaven and God; Author and God; Author a prophet? Before Heaven – EXTRA Hints Tips Stories – includes UFOs and Aliens; World Religions Need to Come Together Now; God's Wisdom Shared; Author's Stories; Karen and I are on God's Team, are you? Conflicting Choices and Answers. Author Treated Harshly by some Teachers in Years 11 and 12, allegedly; Loyalty and Justice; 21+(1 or 2?) Revelations: 32 Stories to Help Prepare Us to Go Home to God; 10 Essential Appendices; 52+ Answers to Reader's Questions; 100+ informed messages from God. 180+ short stories, articles, answers, themes, etc.

God's Gifts to Each of Us

+ We Need to Develop Our Responsibility in Return.

All of us are gifted in very special ways by God, deliberately.

It is our major responsibility *to use our gifts from God and of God's creations, in whatever way we can to assist God and our communities.*

The sorts of gifts we have, include:

Truthfulness

Don't be Greedy

Spirituality and Prayerfulness

Intelligence & Cognitive skills

Compassion

Leadership

Beauty (internal and outwards) and Humour

Physical prowess

Presentation / Education skills

Creative endeavours eg., art, dance, acting

True, genuine, authentic Love Shared

Loyalty

Genuinness and Authenticity

Defender / Defender of the Faith

Effort given for success

Author's – Top 22 Revelations and Discerned Inspired Messages for Today's World.

What Revelations (R) and Discerned Inspired Messages (IM) received by me from God, do I believe are the most appropriate for Today's People Worldwide, now that the Series is completed? Most of these listed below have occurred within the past decade.

1. **R. I, the author, received 21+1 (or +2?) Revelations directly from God in 1982, 2016, 2018, + 2022/3.** These Revelations (R), plus other Discerned Inspired Messages (IM) from God, form the basis of this 10 book series, *'God Today' Series.* Written 2016 to 2023.

2. **R. One God Only for Eternity!** Each religion these days worships the same God, eventhough thinking it is their one and only God!

3. **IM. One Religion Only for all People for Eternity.** The One and Only God leads and guides all people and each Religion. There is now a transition required from God for Only One Religion for All People forever.

4. **R. All people worldwide are Equal, and One before our One and Only God of Eternity.** No matter our differing circumstances, we are all seen as fully equal before God. People who choose to sin are freely moving away from God! Grave sin moves us much further away from God. Genuine Forgiveness sort, brings us back to God.

5. **R. God is Absolute LOVE!**

6. **IM. All Created People, Flora, and Fauna can be with GOD** after 'their' deaths, as discerned by this book's author over many years. All have souls. This is a significant challenge that various religions will be asked to explain to their followers over time. SOULS=LIFE. Love is the Meaning of Life (Especially God's Love). Even non-life inert objects could go to Heaven. More details from God needed on all these possibly qualifying for Heaven. There is also a possibility that God created inert objects may also be in Heaven.

7. **IM. GOD uses Signs** to attract us and help us progress positively to Salvation. Various signs the author received since 2018 are – the large Easter SUN Cross in the sky near Texas, Queensland on the NSW side of the border; SUN flares, sun arrows, sunrays going across me, at heart and brain angles, from the sun sparkling through rainforest canopy; along with going over a published book in this Series that I handheld; all at various treed locations; SUN rays in a cloud going sideways and vertical above Mt Warning; and a double rainbow above my caravan at Amity Point, Straddie, North Stradbroke Island. See Book 4 for the UNIQUE images from GOD – you will be much more than just pleasantly surprised. Each was taken by author. **(***Book 4 is the author's favourite in this Series. Be Truly Amazed!!! Spectacular UNIQUE images from God and stories to share. ***)**

8. **IM**. Aayan Ali's strong proposition for **Islam to have its own Reformation** and/or **Renaissance,** similar to the western world's historical experiences of these, is very much needed for world peace and for literally far less violence. See Ali's 2015 book, *Heretic: Why Islam Needs a Reformation Now.* Ali was Somali born. Her family moved to Saudi Arabia, then escaped to the Netherlands where Aayan became a politician. This was followed by her move to the USA and Harvard University, where she excels as a leader and former Muslim.

9. **R. God seems to have invited me, the author, to be a Prophet of His.** A statement was included in 2016 on the 15 Revelations page, but set differently to the other (R). Appeared like this:

> "I am a prophet
> Prophets are true"

He sent this at 3am in a morning in winter. However, it meant little to me until 3 years later when it became very apparent that it was time for me to consider the invite. I am still in two minds though: being a prophet or not. We aren't to accept God's messages to us blindly. Various people and groups do try to confuse people and act with evil intent. We need to have a high level of acceptance of God's requests, for these to be the Truth. I am tending towards being a Prophet considering God's (R) and (IM) sent over the years. Either way though, God requires me to assist with getting His Revelations and Inspired Messages out to as many people as possible, especially various religious scholars, theologians, leaders, from authentic religions worldwide.

10. **R. God's given us a number of physical methods of proof to know His contact with us is the Truth.** From my experience the key ones are: **Revelations directly to various people** worldwide. **'Tears from God'**, not sobbing crying though, but a flow of tears; **body warmth** from head to toe as during **my experience of being prayed over** starting with hands on my head from Sr Ann, secondary school principal and a charismatic religious sister; **Photographic images** of **various formations from the sun**, e.g. a huge Easter **sun cross** in the sky (cover of Book 4), **sun flares, sun rays** from clouds (cover of Book 2), **sun arrows, cloud** formations, **double rainbows** and **moonrises**. Many of these are from selfie formations, often unseen until uploaded to a PC.

11. **R. Jesus and Mahomad are both God Incarnate** ie. both were fully God and fully man in different eras and countries historically. Book 5, *Jesus and Mahomad are God*, explains the details. An introductory experience for major Incarnations in 2022 (R) or (IM)?

12. **IM. Science and Technology are gifts from God** for us to discover what God's creations are, and what each was created. To then use this new-found knowledge for the betterment of humanity, our Earth, and all other creations.

13. **R. Revelations 1 and 2 from 2016** to the author are so important in a world which seems to becoming so much more fake as time goes on. **Rev. 1. 'Be Truthful' and Rev. 2. 'Don't be Greedy'** lean heavily towards getting our world back to the essential Truths and attitudes for a decent society, which considers each person being valued and as very important as each other equally. Incidentally, you may hear or see both these concepts noted outwardly in today's world. We need Truth and Generosity.

14. **IM.** There is **one last chance to choose God**, i.e., at death, otherwise those who know God and reject God lose out to evil and gain Hell! So much depends on each person's lifestyle, Love or Evil, and beliefs, etc., while on Earth. People who know of God and about God but still reject God outright are mostly destined for Hell.

15. **IM** Discerned **Inspired Messages** from God are given over decades to Bryan Foster, author. And no doubt to others worldwide as well.

16. **R.** We NEED to **NEED GOD and be Vulnerable** to GOD out of the deepest of respect and admittance of the Absolute Godly power over creation and life, being from the one and only Creator, Perfection, and Powerful, well beyond our human understanding. We acknowledge GOD's LOVE and place as being so outside what we could ever imagine but being Absolute Love for each of us. The invitation for each of us is to agree and respond positively every day to our NEEDS

through GOD being essential. Don't ignore God or God's possibilities. Show the legitimate and real NEED you have. Live your absolute and abiding Love for and with God.

17. **IM. GOD's Love is the Meaning of Life**. Continually ask God for this Love throughout your lifetime. Thank God whenever possible, especially when this love is shared with you and others!

18. **IM.** The western first World, should have another Reformation and/or Renaissance for its **generally unholy, secular emphasis.** GOD is missing way too much in the critical world and life decisions. The western world is turning away from GOD. We NEED GOD like never before.

19. **R. Fear rules – often from the cyberworld eliminate this. Cyberbullying - in all its forms, of all sorts, of all ages… needs to be stopped**. This includes for all ages of people, from all countries, all religions, all situations, etc. These **two Revelations #13 and #14 from 2016 when this cyberbullying wasn't as prominent, are being requested now in 2023.** The **cyberworld is impacting on us more negatively now and needs to be sorted** out by the good people of our planet. Along with the assistance of God's Absolute Love.

20. **R., IM. Or nothing? At the end of last year, (Dec. 2022) God sent a Massive Revelation (R) or (IM), so called, due to its huge request for our belief!**

Being from God it is an Absolute Truth, and one which we must believe. Yet, if it wasn't a Revelation (R), it could be a Discerned Inspired Message (IM). We don't need to accept everything which is supposedly from God. We need to verify these as best we can. My first stop for verification are the 'Tears from God'. And these were strongly present. This (R) or (IM) or nothing, appears to have been held back by God until the last moment in the writing of this Book 9. If it is true, then half of the world's population is Incaranted with God, **4 000 000 000 of the 8 000 000 000 people on earth today, are Incarnates with God. Or any other combination fully with God e.g. angels and prophets. What a most incredible divine claim, is this Truth, as revealed by God to us, this time through me the author,** and no doubt other faithful worldwide. **This reality must very strongly help all the 4 billion people who now have with them God Incarnate, for their earthly lives.** How much more support do we really need, if this is so? How incredible is this Major Truth? Yet, are these 4 000 000 000 people informed about this now? If not, informed people, prophets, Angels, etc., should be informing people of their new reality and opportunities. This divine message has come from the One and Only Absolutely Loving God of Eternity. God has gifted us His Absolute Love and as such will guide us to Salvation in His Heaven. **This now links us incredibly close to God throughout our lives, and hence at our death also. We should be incredibly close to God at death! Now we must begin our reality and do as God requires of us.**

21. **IM. Beauty. God's gift to people throughout history.** But what could it be for, before death? Types of beauty.
    See a following detailed article on 'Beauty, God and Us'.

    (See next page 201.)

22. **IM. God. Angels. Feathers - An Overview.**
    Being inspired by others over these past six years who very much believe in angels, has drawn me into an unexpected reality, which I now believe is true. Even down to the use of feathers for communication with humanity. White feathers mostly, are now being seen by me quite often.

    (See page 210.)

*Before **Heaven**: Hints Tips Stories*
Bryan Foster

Beauty, God, and Us

I am one of those who feels aware that I have been extremely fortunate for having been surrounded by beauty, all types of beauty, all my life. Why is it so? God-given Beauty requires an appreciation by the receiver of this unique quality they possess and realise the responsibility they now have for assistance with God's requirements on Earth for and with all of His creation. All this is needed B*efore Heaven*.

Let's start with God. Obviously, without question, God is Absolute BEAUTY – in fact, totally beyond our comprehension. And what beauty He is! Being non-physical, His beauty is very difficult to appreciate and comprehend. Our understanding of beauty is so infinitesimal, so minimal compared with God's beauty, that it almost feels unethical to try and appreciate God beyond our minor undivine sense of beauty! Yet, we must! As with most things, Earth and humanity live within the 'Just before Heaven' locality. That we are so fortunate as to sample and actually live, so much that is necessary for a complete understanding of who and what the absolutely Loving God truly is; and is possible for us all to experience and become a necessary part of this most beautiful experience of absolute divine beauty. We could rightly extrapolate, I believe, that God's beauty is on a level well above earthly creatures, and being non-physical, the physical beauty here is somehow connected with God's beauty, due to the 'importance' humanity places on this. Our understanding of everything about life, love, humanity and God, and everything else, comes from God. So do all the forms of beauty which all creation beholds and lives out or is based upon. Everyone has some form of beauty, at least, even if it doesn't include physical beauty. Don't forget that beauty is in the eye of the beholder. Meaning, somebody is physically beautiful to someone else, but not necessarily to others.

Because our God is absolute divine beauty, well beyond our appreciation of such a quality, we need to work harder towards a better and fuller understanding of this level of beauty. God is not human or physical, therefore God's beauty is both typically physical (Jesus is the incarnated Earthly God.) in our sense of physical beauty and divinely physically beautiful, which is on the God-level, well beyond our reality of physical beauty. It appears that God gives beauty in so many ways, e.g., spiritual, physical, intellectual, emotional, etc.; along when many examples.

Beautiful people physically are attractive and seen as somewhat different and often on a higher level than the average human, even though God has stated that we are all equal, until we move away from God's love freely. These people are often seen as beyond the scope of many people. Hence, these beautiful people have the opportunity to assist God in influencing humanity with God's requirements. A major and necessary purpose for these gifted people.

Most of the population, I feel, very much enjoys the beauty of sincere and genuine people who are fortunately beautiful physically. Other people have incredible, and in many cases, life-long stunning physical beauty. I believe all the people who have special beauty physically, along with those who have beautiful cognitive intelligence, emotional sincerity and compassion, and all other forms of beauty are gifted by God and should realise that their circumstances place them in privileged positions within their religions, families, communities, and society. These groups then need them to see that they also have very special

*Before **Heaven**: Hints Tips Stories*
Bryan Foster

responsibilities from God for themselves and humanity overall. God needs these people to act on His behalf and with Him to help all people realise and learn how to become better people individually and within their societies. These improvements for God's people, help these people on their progression to be with God in Heaven at their deaths. God's main purpose with His creations, is to assist these people to develop their lives in such a way before Heaven, that they end up with life forever in Heaven after their deaths.

This has been my personal aim for decades. Is it yours? That is to be the best sort of God-loving, forgiving, and compassionate person life-long I can be. Even allowing for the weaknesses of humanity and me as a member of humanity, to assist religions, family, friends, communities, and society as a whole, to understand God's expectations and requirements, so as to live in Heaven with God after death, forever.

What, exactly, have I discovered about beauty, which makes me so genuinely understanding of its concept and reality and how it fits in with God and God's people and other creations? Basically, who do I think I am, making such claims about God and God's concept of beauty, especially physical beauty? And the place of humanity in God's Earthly realm?

I am the first to admit that a person's physical beauty is wonderful and could become something extremely special and rewarding for many who have this very special gift from God! It can also be a major hindrance for them and others. A real challenge on how to be yourself in what may be such difficult situations. Being often the centre of attention within groups, or on their own within different communities, can really challenge these people.

Before **Heaven**: *Hints Tips Stories*
Bryan Foster

Being beautiful and attractive is something very special from God, but this can also lead to loneliness and relationship difficulties in beautiful people relating to other people, especially to those who are envious and jealous of beautiful people.

Trying very hard to be the best person we can be within our society isn't easy, especially when surrounded by selfish, jealous, immature adults, who for some reason, believe it is their 'duty' to make the life of beautiful people as difficult as possible. This evil response to God's creations is very difficult at times to even understand?! These people need to mature so as to realise that all people are beautiful in some way, even if not with physical beauty. The loving, caring, empathetic people within our societies are literally a Godsend! The world's intellectual geniuses help humanity immeasurably with their inventions, explanations, etc. As an example, they help create a better world through various scientific, engineering, and technical developments, etc.

I have been incredibly fortunate to have been surrounded and supported by numerous beautiful people. Not just physically beautiful but genuinely beautiful, intelligent, and compassionate family, friends, and beyond; from my wife's family and my family. When families' genuine, loving, authentically beautiful people work together, live together, celebrate together, solve problems together, etc. together over their lifetimes, it becomes a case of beautiful people can definitely be beautiful, intelligent, loving individuals. Considering others should be an essential trait of these people. Within my wife's and my two families, there is physical beauty, but oh so much more beyond the physical when looked into carefully. Many are teachers of children, a noble occupation and necessary for successful

Before *Heaven*: Hints Tips Stories
Bryan Foster

communities. Some are scientists, with one in particular who designed the carbon footprint modelling and details for a recent Australian PM, while working in the CSIRO, Australia's scientific department for science. There are those who are presently, or just in recent times, have become high-quality mothers, at-home mums and mums who work for their families.

This next section is quite difficult to comment on or compare. I am just going to jump in and explore the beauty I see every day in our world. This is the standard section where people reject or challenge what they read and see about beauty, usually out of jealousy, disbelief, commenting, 'Why did I miss out?', and so on. By the way, this reaction and similar, are mostly understood. Especially when our world pushes this aspect of physical beauty in almost all aspects of life. Hence, how could someone who is not beautiful supposedly react to this, as they seem to observe that most of the good things in life seem to end up with the beautiful and/or wealthy ones? Does it really though? Also, there are the 'Who do they think they are?', 'What have I done to be left out of the beauty 'contest'?" Beauty isn't important unless it is being used the correct way to assist God and all others and non-human creations in need. No matter what people think personally, or desire to be the true reality, or invest in, e.g., plastic surgery, beauty isn't anything like people often think it is or the influence it seems to have on so many. I will now share some personal experiences and thoughts on my appearance, and my reaction to others and their inputs in different ways.

Let's begin by remembering that beauty is in the eye of the beholder. How often has this been stated, mostly to help those without copious amounts of physical beauty? But it is so true! We all have at least some, if not many forms of beauty, which

Before **Heaven**: *Hints Tips Stories*
Bryan Foster

we can use to help others worldwide, especially those within our families, communities, and society. All previously mentioned types of beauty are shared around by God with all people on this Earth. Unfortunately, many people don't wish to use these characteristics for good, why? All people have a chance to develop their special beauty with others to help make this a more improved, and highly loving, world of beauty – of all sorts. These people should gain so much personal worth and reward for this assistance. They are on God's side when acting and believing this way.

Now the tough stuff for all those sharing their thoughts along with various ones from God too, on this topic. For simplicity at this stage, it is only me sharing here. It is in the belief that I may have something to offer interested people, that I will try the difficult share. Like many others, I have times in my life when I, and no doubt many others throughout our world, have been told on various occasions that we have nice, friendly personalities, along with other compliments. Yes, it is nice and special when people do/say this to you, or to others who then share it with you, especially when speaking about someone else, who should even benefit from this for their own development. How we react is the most important aspect of this sharing. I have, I believe, successfully tried as best as I can all my life to not let this God-given gift make me any better than anyone else. Having beautiful personal characteristics doesn't make you one iota better than anyone else. No matter what they say or do. There are times when people go overboard with how you look and play up the positive looks and appearance. At times, the best thing to do is to thank them, smile, and then change the topic or move away to stop the often overreaction, which some people feel is the best reaction they could do. This must be done respectfully out of kindness, courtesy, and care for these others. Physically beautiful people can also suffer due to their physical beauty. Nothing in this world is truly free. Beauty also comes at a cost in various ways. The secret is Love for all people, when possible. Genuine, authentic, God taught Love.

I have been incredibly fortunate and appreciative, to be able to genuinely acknowledge God's part in all this. Beauty is a God-given gift. I believe it is usually given as a means for physically attractive people, along with others with other types of beauty, to work with God, to share their gift/s with others, as they try to help bring other people to God. Sharing beauty through your presence with others, gives many of them joy and a positive approach to sharing their gifts with others, all in the name of a far more loving world. This concept of using our gifts for God *Before Heaven*, and for the Love of God and all God's people, is believed to be authentic. I believe this to be an Inspired Message (IM) from God received over many years.

On the other end of this topic, various people who are physically beautiful can find that life may be quite difficult due to this major difference of theirs within our society. Many 'non-beautiful people' become innately jealous of beautiful people. In a world that very much favours beauty for personal acknowledgment, social, career, school, etc. success, and involvement in the good things in life, become too serious and upsetting for beautiful people, especially for those less capable of working through their beauty to accept and answer others who pressurise them due to their looks, etc.

Often the beautiful people are also the wealthy people, which seems to add to their favouritism in life's advancement and pleasures, etc., for many. Even if not wealthy, other people often decide that they must be wealthy too, due to their beauty. This adds to the difficulty of being beautiful. There is a common belief that wealthy people are mostly beautiful people because beauty attracts beauty. With the wealthy attracting the beautiful, and the beautiful attracting the wealthy, often the now wealthy parents bare physically beautiful children.

Even with all this pressure of being beautiful and also often perceived as being wealthy too, God has gifted beautiful people in particular, with various desired physical attributes. These people are then expected by God to use these extra special gifts to work with God on improving the world for all people, no matter the people's gifts, skills, and love for others. They are only beautiful because of God's desire for them and not their own personal actions. They never earned this physical beauty. It was a gift. Genetics assists people with their beauty. God works through the genes of his creations. Any beautiful people who treat their gifts and God with disdain and ignore God's special place and directions for these people, and show off, brag, or treat others with disdain, putting people down, etc., and all the while building themselves up for something these now greedy people, somehow feel is necessary for them to do is so wrong! Why is this so?

The greater the secularism and atheism, the more non-religious, non-God decisions are made by people, and the worse people and the world as a whole become! Many people are challenged by God to be beautiful, and helpful, and to be examples of the greatness of humanity; not to just strut around imagining they have so much to gain from the often-selfish world in which they live. They should be aware that they are charged by God to improve themselves initially, and then various relationships,

*Before **Heaven**: Hints Tips Stories*
Bryan Foster

communities, individuals needing various types of help, religious beliefs, the place of God in the world, etc.

Secular, non-religious, and non-God people, can tend to pull people down easier than most religious people. This is a finding most people seem to agree upon, given the emphasis religions have on Love, and loving relationships, especially with God, family, and other religious people. Of course, secular people also can Love highly, especially with family and friends. The main difference is the place of God seen by each group. Many secular people see the emphasis mainly on them and their family, along with others of like minds, beliefs, and lifestyles in their world. The missing necessity is God's help with and for them. God desires to help everyone equally and immensely, no matter their beliefs, lifestyles, etc. It is up to each person's beliefs and involvement with God, to create their best selves with God's help, compassion, forgiveness, and absolute Love for everyone.

People turn away from God, God doesn't turn away from them. God strongly desires for people to move to Him and live according to His teachings, as much as possible, B*efore Heaven* at death. Divinity is Absolute Bliss! The closer we get to God, the closer we get to Perfection and Absolute Bliss, along with God's Absolute Divine Love and Forgiveness helping us incredibly strongly along the way. As we continue to grow so much closer to God, so much of God's divinity and absolute Love becomes part of us. This continues until our death. At death, people in this situation transition from our now more perfect lives to One of Perfection with God in Heaven. Secular people will mostly argue with me on this point of divinity. Many would see no difference between secular and religious people, even though the difference is quite remarkable in all actuality, once properly understood and appreciated. For the secular, God either doesn't exist, or if God does exist, God isn't something important to the secular. Religion isn't important either.

People who feel asking God for assistance is a sign of weakness, have totally missed the key point. It is through our Need to allow God into our lives, that our showing of our Need, Respect and Vulnerability to God, of God's guidance, of God's Absolute Love is extremely important. Due to God's incredible and total power we must be Real. No faking. This is IT!!!

What do you think?

God. Angels. Feathers. An Overview.

Feathers? Over the past few years, I have been happily drawn to our Australian birds and their songs of beauty, e.g., kookaburras and magpies, but also of their squeals and loud, rough, bird calls, coming from the gold crested cockatoos. Yet, these noisy, screaming white birds, the cockatoos, are still my favourite. They are incredibly beautiful birds who live together in what look like families and flocks. I can certainly appreciate St Kevin's and St Francis' love of birds centuries ago.

During some research, I found that white feathers are left for various people for various reasons. If you combine this with my findings on Angels, a strong link seems to develop. Angels have 'feathers' supposedly. They also apparently send us signs through their feathers. Archangel Michael has white feathers. He leaves these at places where he has helped or is helping someone with their difficulties within this life. Or for encouraging people to do what God needs done for people, communities, and societies. He is giving major support and assistance to these people.

I have regularly, these days, come across these feathers. The colours of the ones I come across are mostly white, but also brownish and brown-greenish. I have legitimately found that peace immediately descends over me through these discoveries. Sometimes I even feel very much charged with a call to work with God closely and receive peace, safety, and love from God.

Even though this seems quite a challenge for others, and myself at times, I am strongly beginning to see this sign as one of God's legitimate presences with me and the circumstances in which I find myself. I can certainly imagine that many others should find themselves in similar situations as me. It is what we do with this newfound wisdom and knowledge that decides our help with God's earthly future.

What do you think?

*Before **Heaven**: Hints Tips Stories*
Bryan Foster

AUTHOR'S PUBLICATIONS

'GOD TODAY' SERIES, Books 1-10 by Bryan Foster, 2016-23

This is a series of ten nonfiction books, including eight textbooks and two photobooks, plus a video series by Bryan Foster. All released between 2016 and 2023. 21+(3) Revelations from 1982, 2016, 2018, 2022/3, plus numerous Discerned Inspired Messages going back decades, formed the background for these 10 books and Video Series.

Book 1. *1GOD.world: One GOD for All,* (Author Articles) (2016)

Book 2. *Mt Warning GOD's Revelation: Photobook Companion to '1GOD.world',* (2017)

Book 3. *Where's GOD? Revelations Today,* (Author Articles) (2018)

Book 4. *Where's GOD? Revelations Today Photobook Companion: GOD Signs (2nd ed)* (2018). Images So Unique and God-Given!

Book 5. *Jesus and Mahomad are GOD* (Author Articles) (2020)

Book 6. *Love is the Meaning of Life: GOD'S Love (1st ed)* (2021)

Book 7. *Wisdom: GOD's Hints and Tips (Author Articles)* (2021)

Book 8 (8A and B). *Love is the Meaning of Life (1st ed)* (2022) Book 8. *Love is the Meaning of Life* (for Secular People) (1st ed) (Book 8 is an edited version of the 2ⁿᵈ ed. i.e., Book 6, 2021, and includes an introduction to God's Love for the non-believer and those with doubts. It includes an introduction to God's Love for the non-believer and those with doubts.

Book 9. *Before Heaven: Major Challenges from God* (2023)

Book 10. B*efore Heaven: Hints Tips Stories (2ⁿᵈ ed)* (2023)

Author's Photobooks

My Australia Photobooks Series – 12 x photobooks of Northern Territory and (FNQ) Far North Queensland, (2014-5)

Mt Warning Wollumbin Circuit: a Photographic Journey, (2018)

'Straddie' North Stradbroke Island: Photobook of Natural & Shared Beauty, (2019)

'*God Today' Series,* 2 photobooks - #s 2 and 4 (2016 - 2023) - *Mt Warning GOD's Revelation: Photobook Companion to '1GOD.world',* (2017)

Where's GOD? Revelations Today Photobook Companion: GOD Signs (2nd ed) (2018). Images So Unique and God-Given!

*Before **Heaven**: Hints Tips Stories*
Bryan Foster

Author's Marketing Books

School Marketing for the Digital Age, (3rd ed), 2011

Church Marketing for the Digital Age, (2nd ed), 2011

Author's Video Series.

YouTube 780+ videos (free at this stage) - (User names/channels - efozz1 or CaravanAus)

'God Today' Series, 30+ videos

'How to...' for those beginner caravanners + *Places to stay, things to see and do while caravanning throughout Australia.* (30+ now)

+ PUBLISHED ACADEMIC JOURNAL ARTICLES

*Before **Heaven**: Hints Tips Stories*
Bryan Foster

AUTHOR'S WEBSITES

https://www.godtodayseries.com/ (Main website for this series, includes the blog commenced in 2016)

https://www.jesusandmahomadaregod.com/ (Book 5's website – being developed)

https://www.bryanfosterauthor.com (Author's website)

http://www.greatdevelopmentspublishers.com/ (Incl. Publisher's new webpage. Original website started in 2007, ended 12/2018.)

https://www.facebook.com/groups/38960269805146/ (God Today, Facebook)

https://au.linkedin.com/in/(bryanfoster - LinkedIn)

https://www.youtube.com/user/efozz1 (780+ Free YouTube videos. Any cost changes will be advised prior. Commenced video production in 2009.)

https://twitter.com/1Godworld1 (Twitter – being developed)

https://www.instagram.com/ (Instagram – God world – being developed). *Love is the Meaning of Life* (for Secular People) (1st ed) Book 8. (An edited version – includes an introduction to God's Love for the non-believer and those with doubts.)

Before **Heaven**: *Hints Tips Stories*
Bryan Foster

Overview of Author

Bryan Foster graduated with a MEd (Religious Education) from Australian Catholic University in Sydney and Brisbane. He was a religious school and parish leader before retirement. A retired teacher of 42 years is now primarily a religious/spirituality non-fiction book author, editor, publisher, photographer, and videographer. Bryan taught the Study of Religion for 30 years to years 11 and 12 students in Brisbane and the Gold Coast. In addition, he has been a primary/elementary Catholic school principal in southern Queensland (twice), at Tara and Goondiwindi, and an assistant principal of religious education (and pastoral care) at Aquinas College, a secondary college on the Gold Coast (for 12 years).

Church wise, Bryan was the chair and secretary of both diocesan and parish pastoral councils, in the Gold Coast and southern Brisbane archdiocese. He is married to Karen with three adult children and four grandchildren. Bryan has professionally published academic religious education journal articles, along with five school and church marketing books. Interests include:

1. 10 books in the *'God Today' Series*. (2016-2023)

2. A YouTube channel for the *'God Today' Series* at efozz1. (2016)

3. Five Marketing School and Church books. (2009-2011)

4. A YouTube channel for caravan/trailer beginners (CaravanAus or efozz1). Also published a travel article in an Australian caravan and camping magazine, as a freelance journalist. (2009-)

5. Videos for caravanners, concentrating on places to stay and things to do and see throughout Australia. (2012-)

There are 780+ free (at this stage) videos covering these themes, along with photobooks for 'RVers', 12 Around Australia books + numerous videos, etc.

Bryan has been writing and publishing books, videos and websites since 2007. An overview of most publications was listed four pages previously. Karen, his wife, and he, are both directors of their private publishing company, Great Developments Publishers. Karen assists with editing and photography.

Academic Qualifications:

MEd Australian Catholic University, (ACU), Sydney and Brisbane

BEd, (ACU), Brisbane

Grad. Dip. RE (ACU) Brisbane

Dip..RE. (Institute of Faith), Brisbane

Dip T (McAuley Teachers College), Brisbane

Books by Bryan and Karen are available for purchase at Internet Bookstores and Various Bookstore Fronts Worldwide.

Before **Heaven**: *Hints Tips Stories*
Bryan Foster

Published by

Great Developments Pty Ltd.

Trading as

Great Developments Publishers

Gold Coast, Queensland, Australia.

(Bryan W. Foster and Karen M. Foster – Directors)

info@greatdevelopmentspublishers.com

bryanwfoster@gmail.com

All Publications are Copyright © 2007 - 2023 Great Developments Publishers, Bryan W. Foster and Karen M. Foster – Directors

ACN: 33435168 ABN: 13133435168 USA-EIN: 98-0689457

Gold Coast, Queensland, Australia

https://www.BryanFosterAuthor.com

https://www.GodTodaySeries.com(14) God Today | Facebook

*Before **Heaven**: Hints Tips Stories*
Bryan Foster

*Before **Heaven**: Hints Tips Stories*
Bryan Foster

www.ingramcontent.com/pod-product-compliance
Lightning Source LLC
Chambersburg PA
CBHW051429290426
44109CB00016B/1489